KT-558-176

500

Internet

Hints, Tips, and Techniques

114629

053298

THE HENLEY COLLEGE LIBRARY

A RotoVision Book
Published and distributed by RotoVision SA
Route Suisse 9, CH-1295 Mies
Switzerland

RotoVision SA, Sales & Editorial Office
Sheridan House, 114 Western Road
Hove BN3 1DD, UK

Tel: +44 (0)1273 72 72 68
Fax: +44 (0)1273 72 72 69
Email: sales@rotovision.com
Web: www.rotovision.com

Copyright © RotoVision SA 2008

All rights reserved. No part of this publication
may be reproduced, stored in a retrieval system,
or transmitted in any form or by any means,
electronic, mechanical, photocopying, recording,
or otherwise, without permission of the
copyright holder.

10 9 8 7 6 5 4 3 2 1

ISBN: 978-2-940378-41-8

Designed by Studio Ink
Art Director: Jane Waterhouse

Reprographics in Singapore by ProVision (Pte) Ltd.
Tel: +65 6334 7720
Fax: +65 6334 7721

Printed in Singapore by Star Standard Industries (Pte) Ltd.

500

Internet

Hints, Tips, and Techniques

The Easy, All-in-One Guide to those Inside
Secrets for Blogging, Vlogging, Photologging,
Facebook, YouTube, Flickr, and more

Dan Oliver

Contents

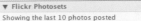

Browse Better

Blogger

Facebook

Flickr

YouTube

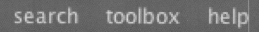

Keep In Touch

Get Organized

Get Paid

Introduction

It's easy to feel like you're always playing catch up on the web. New sites and services seem to be launching on a daily basis, and it's difficult to identify those that you should be using, and those that you should be avoiding like the plague; that's where *500 Internet Hints, Tips, and Techniques* is going to help you out.

I'm going to show you how you can harness the internet to its fullest potential and make it work for you. It doesn't matter whether you're new to the web, or whether you've been online for years, this book will help you browse better and smarter, and I'll reveal some of the great new sites and web applications that you can't afford to miss out on.

The real buzz of the moment surrounds a group of sites and web applications that fall under the umbrella of Web 2.0. The chances are that you've heard this term used in the media and online, but there are various definitions of Web 2.0 and what it actually means. The simplest way to think of Web 2.0 is as a new generation of sites and applications that enable their users to share and collaborate online. Simple, huh? If Web 1.0 was a monologue, then Web 2.0 is the biggest conversation on the planet, and I'll reveal how you can join in!

But why should you take my advice? Well, that's a good question. As a technology journalist who has written about the web for the last decade, I've spent countless hours online sifting through the flotsam and jetsam of the internet. Since 1997 I have edited two internet magazines, written for various newspapers, designed a host of websites, appeared on radio shows and podcasts, and even stood outside Buckingham Palace with a placard promoting one of my sites! (I'm not condoning this, though, as it could get you arrested.) During this time I've written about thousands of websites, and this book features some of the best.

In chapter one, I'll explain the benefits of choosing the right browser, and outline how the right one can open up a plethora of new avenues on the net. Once your browsing needs have been met, I'm going to concentrate on Blogger, and look at how you can publish your very own website with the minimum amount of fuss.

Hopefully, by this point, you'll be ready to get your teeth into some serious Web 2.0 applications, so in chapter three I'll introduce you to Flickr, and reveal the joys of one of the world's largest photography communities. In the next chapter I'll focus specifically on Facebook. Facebook is the fastest growing social network on the planet (according to research from comScore), and it enables you to share video, music, photos, and much more besides. Next up, I'll show you how to get your videos onto the global video community that is YouTube, and you'll also learn how to add them to your own site.

Finally, in the last three chapters of the book, I'll provide tips on how you can communicate better, stay organized, and make money online.

So, whether you want to keep in touch with friends and family; stay up-to-date with the latest news; share video, photos, and audio online; make money from your site; keep an online diary; or simply have some fun, I hope that there's something in this book that you can benefit from.

Let's get started!

Firefox   File   Edit   View   History   Bookmarks   Scrapbook   Tools   Window   Help   ✳ 📶 🔊 🔋 (100%) 🏴 Sat 12:47 🔍

Firefox – Rediscover the Web

http://en-us.www.mozilla.com/en-US/firefox/pgcshort/index.html   ▾ ▷   G ▾ Google   🔍

Getting Started   Latest Headlines

mozilla   Products   Add-ons   Support   Developers   Blog   About

Home » Products » Firefox

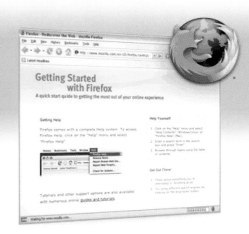

Firefox 2
Simply Powerful.
Powerfully Simple.

See why millions rely on Firefox to browse the web.

✓ Surf more efficiently with tabbed browsing, integrated search, and faster page loading.

✓ Rest easy knowing we block pop-ups, viruses and spyware.

✓ Customize your web experience with more add-ons, visual themes and options than any other browser.

Download Firefox FREE ↓

2.0.0.4 for Mac OS X, English (17.0MB) -
Other Versions

"The bottom line: Mozilla Firefox 2 is a winner, beating Microsoft Internet Explorer 7 on security, features, and overall cool factor."
CNET EDITORS' REVIEW, OCTOBER 2006

Firefox Details:
Features - Awards - System Requirements - Release Notes

http://en-us.www.mozilla.com/products/download.html?product=firefox-2.0.0.4&os=osx&lang=en-US

As far as browsers go, they don't get any better than Firefox.

Blogger isn't just a fantastic blogging platform, it's also free!

With millions of users, MySpace is the world's biggest social network.

Owned by Google, YouTube is the king of internet video.

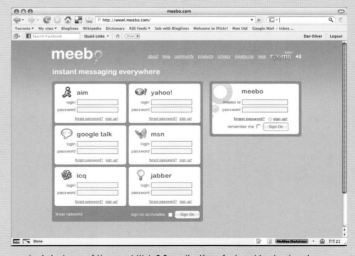

meebo is just one of the great Web 2.0 applications featured in chapter six.

If you want to share your photos online, there's no better site than Flickr.

Browse Better

In this chapter we'll reveal how you can become a better browser. First up, we'll introduce you to Firefox: the browser of choice for discerning internet users. While other browsers such as Opera and Safari have some great features, it's Firefox that offers the most support for third-party add-ons. Next, we'll look at the exciting world of web feeds, and explain how they can save you hours of web browsing, and serve up the latest links from your favorite sites. Last, but by no means least, we'll take a look at del.icio.us, the social bookmarking site that enables you to have more control over your links than ever before and gives you access to them from any computer on the internet.

Firefox features

Kiss Internet Explorer goodbye

Although Microsoft has gone a long way to improving things with its version 7 browser, it still has issues. Internet Explorer (IE) doesn't fully support web standards, and, in contrast, Firefox has thousands of third-party add-ons and a bucketload more features.

You don't have to delete IE

If you're worried that Firefox may not be for you, don't be. You can have both browsers installed on your system at the same time, so there's nothing to stop you downloading Firefox, as it's totally free. (In fact, if you're a developer, then we recommend keeping IE on your system for testing purposes.)

003 Web standards

Today's best sites are built with web standards in mind (see CSS Beauty at www. cssbeauty.com for some great examples). This means that style (in the shape of documents called "style sheets") and content (in the form of XHTML) are created separately, and Firefox handles these sites brilliantly.

004 Get Firefox

Many of you will not be using Firefox as your default browser, but over the next few pages we will explain why—in our opinion—it is currently the best browser available for both Mac and PC users. To install Firefox, go to www.getfirefox.com, and follow the instructions for your operating system.

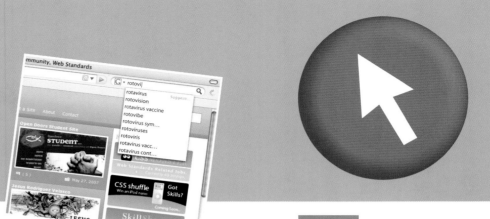

005 Set as default

When you first run Firefox, you'll be greeted with a dialog box, asking whether you want Firefox to be your default browser. You can change this at a later date in your preferences, but for now select "yes" (now any links you select in other applications will open in Firefox by default).

006 The search window

One difference you may notice upon opening Firefox is a search window to the top right. It defaults to Google, but you can add and remove new search engines from the drop-down menu by selecting the arrow on the right of the search window.

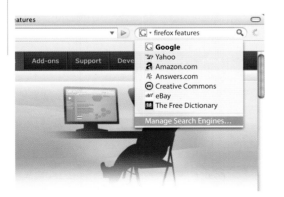

007 A bit more on search

As well as being able to add various search engines to Firefox, you'll notice that when you start to search, Firefox will provide suggestions. If you see what you're looking for in the list, either arrow down to the section or simply select it with your mouse.

008 Browser restore

If you've used Internet Explorer to date, then you're probably used to random crashes! Thankfully, the Firefox developers realize how annoying crashes can be, so whenever Firefox unexpectedly quits—which is rare—you'll be given the choice to restore a previous session.

009 The power of tabs

Tabs make browsing a joy, and enable you to have numerous sites open in one browser window. To open a new tab on a Mac, simply press Command + T (Alt + T on a PC). And if you accidentally close a tab you can get it back by going to History>Recently Closed Tabs.

010 Scrolling through tabs

There will come a point where you may have too many tabs open, and there's a little tip that you can use to jump through your tabs. Just press Ctrl + Tab to scroll from left to right, and Ctrl + Shift + Tab to scroll back to the right.

011 Spell-checking

You can come up with the most intelligent blog or forum post in the world, but if it includes misspelled words you'll look rather stupid! Thankfully, Firefox has a handy spell-checker to save your blushes. If Firefox spots a word that's spelled incorrectly, a red line appears below it and you can then right or Ctrl click to get a list of suggested replacements.

012 Pop-up blocking

Anything that can go some way toward eradicating pop-ups from your online experience is a good thing. When you visit a site with pop-ups in Firefox, a yellow bar appears at the top of the browser. Select the Preferences tab to allow pop-ups, or edit your preferences further.

013 Avoid phishing scams

Identity theft is becoming a major problem on the net, with "phishing" sites set up to try and dupe you into providing personal details, which can then be used to steal your money. Firefox keeps a list of suspected phishing sites, and when you visit one of them, a warning window will display.

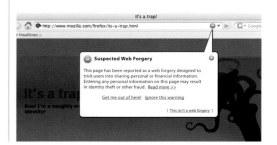

014 Clear private data

In the past, browsers have kept information on your browsing habits, even when you thought they'd been deleted. Firefox clears all your private data via one handy button. Simply go to Tools>Clear Private Data and select Clear Private Data Now.

015 Find stuff

Press Ctrl + F on a PC (Command + F on a Mac) and a Find bar appears at the bottom of your browser. Start typing the word you're looking for, and Firefox will jump to the first instance of that word on the page. Find will even work with text within frames.

016 Bookmarks basics

When you're on a page that you'd like to add to your bookmarks, simply press Command + D on a Mac (or Ctrl + D on a PC) and the Bookmarks window will open. You will then be able to add the site to your main Bookmarks or the Bookmarks Toolbar (a bar always visible at the top of your browser).

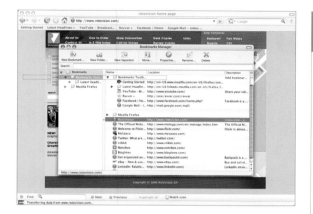

018 The Bookmarks Toolbar

To have bookmarks appear in the Bookmarks Toolbar—and therefore always visible in your browser—just drag them into the Bookmarks Toolbar folder. You should reserve this space for sites you visit on a daily basis.

017 Manage bookmarks

To open the Bookmarks Manager go to Bookmarks>Organize Bookmarks, and this will open a new window. In this window you'll see your bookmarks in the main section of the interface, tabs running along the top, and folders down the left.

019 Take the Toolbar further

You'll find the Toolbar gets full very quickly. To get around this you can create folders within the Toolbar, which will display as drop-downs. Create a new folder and place links in it that have something in common with each other, such as sites that show videos. Now select the main Bookmarks folder, and drag your new folder from the main window into the Bookmarks Toolbar folder. It will now show up as a drop-down menu in your Toolbar.

020 Amazing add-ons

Possibly the best feature of Firefox is the ability to install add-ons. These are little bits of software that add extra functionality to your browser. Go to https://addons.mozilla.org to find an exhaustive list.

Top Firefox add-ons

There are hundreds of great Firefox add-ons to choose from, but we've whittled them down to 20 of our favorites. Our first 10 add-ons should be of interest to everyone, while our final 10 (on pages 16–17) concentrate on those of you with your own websites. Unless stated otherwise, all add-ons can be found online at https://addons.mozilla.org

021 ScrapBook

This add-on is perfect if you spend a lot of time researching online; it enables you to save "clippings," which can take the form of links, images, text selections, and more.

022 del.icio.us Bookmarks

del.icio.us (http://del.icio.us) is a great site for storing bookmarks online, so any computer connected to the net can access them easily (we'll look at del.icio.us in more detail later in this chapter). With del.icio.us Bookmarks you can easily add and manage links via Firefox, with new tabs added to your browser interface.

023 ColorfulTabs

The Firefox interface looks pretty good as it is, but if you'd like to color up your tabs, then ColorfulTabs is the perfect add-on for you. This is definitely one for the children of the 80s!

024 FoxyTunes

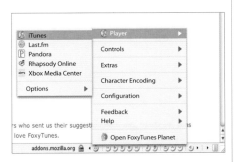

This add-on is a must for music fans. Once installed, FoxyTunes provides you with control of your favorite media player from within your browser, thus ensuring that you don't have to leave your browser when you want to skip to the next track. It also works with online services such as Last.fm and Pandora.

025 McAfee SiteAdvisor

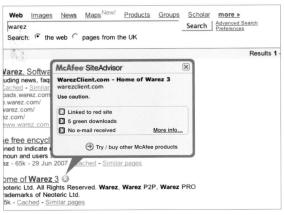

Scammers, spammers, and hackers are doing some very naughty things online, and it's easy to feel vulnerable. Thankfully, the SiteAdvisor team is busy policing the net for us. Install this add-on, which you can get from www.siteadvisor.com, and you can access information on any site you visit or search for. Just hover your mouse over the SiteAdvisor icons when they appear.

026 Mouse Gestures

If moving your mouse to the top of the browser is too much effort—and for many of us, it is!—then this add-on enables you to use mouse gestures to control browser behavior. You can edit the Mouse Gestures preferences by going to Tools>Add-ons and selecting Preferences (you can also print all the supported gestures here).

027 Fotofox

If you currently share photos online via Flickr, Tabblo, 23hq, SmugMug, Marela, or Kodak EasyShare Gallery then Fotofox enables you to simply drag photos into the browser to upload them to your site of choice.

028 Viamatic foXpose

Being able to view all your active tasks at once is something that both Windows Vista and Mac OSX users appreciate, and now you can apply the same tiling to open tabs in Firefox. Just click the foXpose tab at the bottom left of your browser, and behold a treasure trove of tiled tabs.

029 Gspace

If you don't have a Gmail account, then you'll need to sign up at www.gmail.com before you can use this add-on. Once you've done that, you can use your Gmail webspace as online storage. It's a genius idea, and perfect if you often share files between computers.

030 All-in-One Sidebar

Managing all these add-ons can be a pain, so Ingo Wennemaring has designed an add-on to make it easy. Not only can you manage your add-ons, you can also see your browsing history, bookmarks, and downloads.

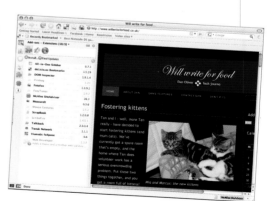

Firefox add-ons: take things further

Whether you maintain a blog or get your hands dirty with more serious web design, these Firefox add-ons will help make your life easier, and save you some precious hours in the process.

031 Measurelt

There are countless times when, as a website designer, you need to measure an element on a web page. Now, thanks to this great add-on from Kevin Freitas, you can get a pixel measurement of anything residing within a web browser. Simply select the ruler icon from the bottom left of the browser, and drag it over the item you want to measure.

032 ScribeFire

WordPress is one of the most popular platforms for bloggers, and ScribeFire is one of the most popular tools for users of WordPress. Install ScribeFire, press F8 (or select the orange pad and pencil at the bottom of the interface), and write your next blog post in the panel that opens up. Simple perfection.

033 Firebug

This may be a little too technical for most people, but if you do any coding with CSS, HTML, and especially JavaScript, then this add-on will be indispensable. Firebug helps you edit, debug, and monitor your code—live!

034 FireFTP

Is there anything Firefox plug-ins can't do? Well, it would appear not, because you can even get this fantastic add-on that enables you to transform Firefox into an FTP client. Once you've added FTP details, you can just drag and drop files, or access a host of great advanced features.

035 Color Contrast Analyzer

Bad contrast doesn't just affect those with poor eyesight, it can also render text illegible to those with color blindness. Color Contrast Analyzer will perform a series of tests on any open site, and can be downloaded at http://juicystudio.com/article/colour-contrast-analyser-firefox-extension.php.

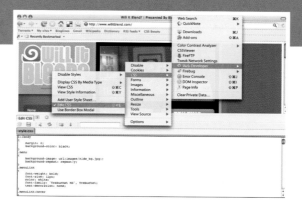

036 ColorZilla

ColorZilla is a simple but immensely useful tool. When you want to find the value of a color, you simply select the dropper icon at the bottom left of your browser, and click on the color. Right-click the dropper, and a host of other features are at your disposal, including the ability to create a "favorites" list of colors.

038 Web Developer

Where most add-ons do one thing well, Web Developer does lots of things brilliantly. Viewed by many as the king of develop add-ons, Chris Pederick's Web Developer enables you to view CSS, edit CSS, validate pages, measure elements, clear session cookies, and much more besides.

037 CSSViewer

Go to Tools>CSSViewer and you'll activate this small, but incredibly useful, add-on. Now you can hover your mouse over any CSS element and see its attributes.

039 IE Tab

This add-on isn't available for Mac users, but is a godsend for those people developing sites on PCs. We all know pages don't always render correctly in Microsoft's Internet Explorer browser, so now you can quickly switch to IE's rendering engine from within Firefox.

040 Greasemonkey

Greasemonkey is an add-on that enables you to use hundreds of small scripts to customize the way websites display. Once you've installed Greasemonkey, simply visit www.greasespot.net to access a plethora of scripts (we'll be using a great script for del.icio.us later in this chapter, see tip 103).

Web feeds explained

One of the best additions to all the major browsers available today is the ability to view and manage web feeds. There are two standards for feeds—RSS and Atom. You don't need to worry about these, but it's good to note that when you see RSS or Atom on a site, they're referring to web feeds. Feeds enable you to keep track of frequently updated content on a site—such as news, blog posts, forums, or schedules—without having to ever visit the website in question (think of them as news tickers that provide a short summary of information, and only take you to a website when you click a headline). To access and manage these feeds you need something called a newsreader; these can be stand-alone programs, web-based applications, or can be built into your web browser. The best way to learn about feeds is to jump in and start using them; we'll now reveal everything you need to know about web feeds, and even show you how to create your own!

041 Spotting a feed

OK, so we've provided a brief introduction to feeds, but how do you find them? Thankfully, there's a standard symbol for web feeds (both RSS and Atom), which is an orange tab, featuring two white waves emanating from the bottom left (you'll also sometimes see "XML" on an orange background). When you see it, there's a web feed in the house; however, be aware that some developers, who love to be different, will just provide a feed link without the standard symbol.

Sport

- **Beckham unfazed by pressure in US**
- Murali captures 700th Test wicket

| Sports feeds

042 Now what?

When you see a feed logo on a site or section of a site that you'd like to be updated about, then you just click on the link or logo. In Firefox this will open a new page, where you will then be asked what you want to do with this feed.

043 Feed alert

Sometimes feeds can be hidden away in the body of a website, but there's an easy way to identify sites with web feeds. When you're on a site and want to subscribe to a feed, simply look on the right side of the address field in Firefox. If you see the orange logo, then there's a feed on the page.

 044 Choose your reader

In this page you'll see a drop-down menu. By default you can choose to add your feed to Firefox's Live Bookmarks—which is what we'll do for now—but you'll also see a number of different options that we'll look at later in this chapter.

045 Live Bookmarks

When you add a feed to Live Bookmarks you'll be asked where you'd like to have it appear (Bookmarks, Bookmarks Toolbar, or any folders you've created already). For now, choose Bookmarks Toolbar. Once you've done this your new feed will appear at the top of the browser.

046 Get your feed anywhere

Now, whatever page you decide to navigate to, you will always be able to access the latest information for any given feed by simply rolling over it with your mouse. However, your Toolbar will quickly fill up, so we're going to manage our feeds.

047 Managing your feeds

Live Bookmarks can quickly fill your Toolbar, so you need to manage them. First, go to Bookmarks>Organize Bookmarks and this will open your Bookmarks Manager. Click in the main window, select the New Folder tab at the top of the interface, and give it a name.

048 Put the feed in the folder

Now, in the main window, drag your new folder into the Bookmarks Toolbar folder. Once you've done this, you can drag all the relevant feeds—which will show up as their own folders—into this folder, and access them via your Bookmarks Toolbar. Whenever you add a new feed, this folder will show up in the drop-down.

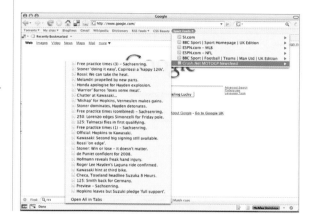

049 What if there's no logo or link?

Sometimes you will just see a link on a site, like this: http://rss.crash.net/crash_6.xml. Don't worry that there's no link or logo. To add it to Live Bookmarks, you just need to copy the link and paste it into your URL field in Firefox, and hit return. You'll then be taken to the feed subscription page.

Manage feeds with Bloglines

Despite the support for web feeds within Firefox, it's great to be able to access your feeds from any PC or Mac, and have more features at your fingertips. To achieve this, we need to use a web-based application such as Bloglines. Here, we'll show you how to manage your feeds with this fantastic online newsreader.

050 Sign up to Bloglines

The first thing you need to do is head over to www.bloglines.com and click the Register link. Now you'll need to add an active email address, and select a password (it's important you use an active email account, as you'll need to verify your account).

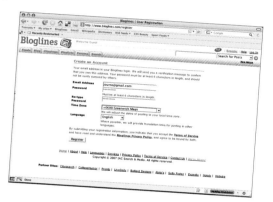

051 The interface

Once you have validated your account, you can start using Bloglines. You'll see that the interface is separated into two panes, with four tabs in the left pane (Feeds, Blog, Clippings, Playlist). Under the feeds tab you'll notice that you're already subscribed to a default feed.

052 Add new feeds—the easy way

Whenever you see a feed link on a site, the first thing you need to do is copy the link. Now select Add within the Feeds section in Bloglines, and paste the feed URL. Select Subscribe, and you'll be taken to the last screen, where you can select settings for the feed (such as which folder it appears in, how the feed will be displayed, and whether it will be public or private).

053 Add new feeds—the easier way

If you've decided to stick with Firefox then there's an even easier way to add feeds. When you see a feed, just select it, choose Bloglines from the drop-down on the feed subscription page, and hit Subscribe Now. You'll now see your new feeds on the left of the interface.

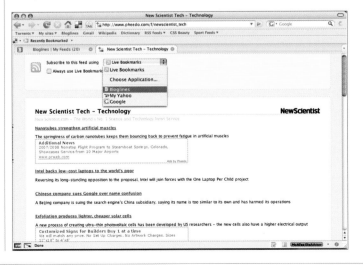

054 Bloglines and Flickr

In chapter three we'll provide you with an in-depth look at the photo phenomenon that is Flickr, but for now we'll just show you how to get an update when someone adds new pictures to their account. Find a Flickr account you would like to monitor, then simply select Add and paste the site URL (for example, http://www.flickr.com/photos/doliver). You can even subscribe to specific tags, by copying the link of a tag in Flickr.

055 The Bookmarklet

Bloglines provides a Bookmarklet, which makes it easy to add feeds. You'll find the Bookmarklet link in the left-hand pane. In the Bookmarklet section you'll see buttons for different browsers, and to install it in Firefox you just need to drag the button onto your Bookmarks Toolbar (there are instructions for other browsers). Now just hit the Sub with Bloglines link to quickly add a feed.

056 Using Bloglines

Now you've added some feeds, we can look more closely at how to use Bloglines. All feeds will show up on the left, and once you've viewed a feed the link will gray out so you can see those that you've read.

057 New folders

As you add more feeds you'll appreciate the need for folders. To add new folders in Bloglines you must first select Edit within the Feeds tab, then select the New Folder link, and finally provide a new folder title in the resulting pop-up. To populate new folders select feeds in the left pane, and drag the relevant ones into your new folder. Whenever you want to make changes in the future, you'll need to enter the Edit section.

058 Search tool

By using the Search tab—in the main section of the Bloglines interface—you can search for new feeds, and even search within posts (just use the drop-down menu to specify your search criteria). The most popular feeds that meet your criteria will be returned first and you'll be able to see how many subscribers the feed has.

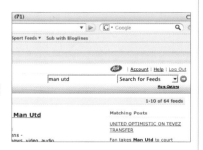

059 Clippings

Now that we've covered the basics in Bloglines, it's time to look at some of the cool features on offer. First up is the Clippings section. Whenever you come across a feed item that you want to keep, you click the Clip/Blog This link, and then select Save to, and choose Clippings folder (you can add extra text if you wish). This item will then be permanently stored within the Clippings tab.

060 Set up a blog

As you have probably already noticed, when you select Clip/Blog This, you can also choose to add the item to a blog. However, you must first create a blog to do this (go into the Blog tab to create your page). You will be asked to provide a username, title, and description for the blog. Also, you must choose if you want to make it available to the public.

061 Publish your clippings

To add an item to your blog, select Publish to Blog–instead of adding the item to your Clippings–and the feed item will be published to your page. Then–within the Blog tab–you can choose View Blog to see your new page.

062 Bloglines email

If you'd like to have all the email newsletters that you subscribe to appear within Bloglines, you can create Bloglines email addresses–which you can then use to sign up to newsletters and the like–and be notified when new mails arrive. Select Create Email Subscriptions from the bottom of the Feeds section, and then enter your desired name for the subscription. A new account will be created, and an email will be generated, which you can use going forward.

063 OPML support

Bloglines supports the OPML format, so you can easily import and export your feeds. Just select Import Subscriptions or Export Subscriptions from the Additional Features menu on the left of the interface.

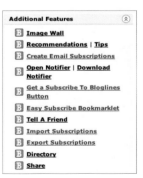

Additional Features

- **Image Wall**
- **Recommendations | Tips**
- **Create Email Subscriptions**
- **Open Notifier | Download Notifier**
- **Get a Subscribe To Bloglines Button**
- **Easy Subscribe Bookmarklet**
- **Tell A Friend**
- **Import Subscriptions**
- **Export Subscriptions**
- **Directory**
- **Share**

064 Holy hotkeys!

One of the things that keeps people coming back to Bloglines is the support for hotkeys. At the bottom of each feed display you'll find a list of the hotkeys, and soon you'll wonder how you ever managed without them!

065 Get notified

Select Open Notifier from the Additional Features menu, and you'll find a number of different ways that you can get notified of new items in your Bloglines account, including extensions for the main web browsers, as well as programs for Mac and PC. You can even get a widget for your Mac Dashboard.

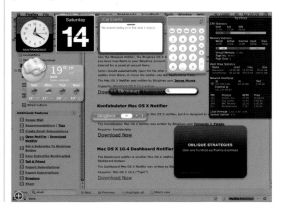

066 Share your feeds

If you'd like to share your feeds with others (known as a blogroll)—and don't mind people finding out about your desire to stay updated with Phil Collins' tour dates—then select Share from the Additional Features. Add your name, what you'd like to display (leave this blank to display all), and hit Generate HTML. JavaScipt is then generated, which can be added to your blog or website.

067 My blogroll won't display!

If your shared feed doesn't display, then you'll need to go into Blog Settings in Bloglines, and select Yes, Publish my Blogroll. Once you've done this, it should display fine.

068 Your secret's still safe

When publishing your blogroll you can select which feeds can be seen by the wider web. If you don't want people to see a specific feed then just remember to select Private within the Access section when adding a new feed.

Create your own feed

One of the best things about feeds is just how easy it is to create them for your own website. There are a number of web-based tools you can use to generate your own feed, but we've opted for IceRocket's RSS Builder at http://rss.icerocket.com.

069 Sign up

Before you can get started you'll have to create an account. Rather than fill your inbox with junk, why not use the Email Subscriptions service in Bloglines, so you can keep all sign-up emails in one handy place. Of course, you can use your standard email to sign up, should you choose to.

071 Create your feed

When you first sign in, you'll be taken to a page, at the top of which is a button that reads Create Channel. Hit that button. On the next screen you'll have to enter general information about your feed, and you can even associate an image with it.

070 Activate your account

If you signed up with your standard email account then you'll need to sign in and visit the link in the activation email from IceRocket. However, if you used a Bloglines email, you can just enter your Bloglines account and find the mail account in the pane on the left (it'll have a little envelope next to it that denotes a mail account).

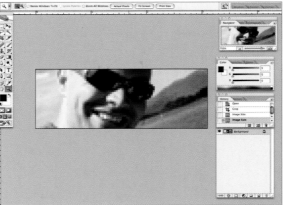

072 Channel image

To give your feed a bit of personality, you can associate a channel image with it (this won't display in all feed aggregators). This element is an optional extra for feeds, and will usually include the logo of the feed owner (or, in this example on the left, a picture of the site's owner on vacation). The default size for the image is 88 pixels wide by 31 pixels high, and will need to be saved in a web-friendly image format (use a JPEG as default).

 073 Upload your image

Once you've created your logo, you'll need to upload it to your webspace and make a note of the URL of the image. You can use the FireFTP Firefox extension to do this (see tip 034). We've placed ours in a folder called Feed.

074 You've created a feed

Having entered your details, you'll be taken to a page that lists your new feed. At the moment your feed has no entries, so subscribers will see a blank feed. To add a new story to your feed, select Add Entry on the right of the screen, and fill in the form.

075 New entries

You will then see your entry displayed on the next page, with a number of links that enable you to modify, publish, and validate your feed. Select Publish, and you'll be provided with a segment of code that you can drop into your site, which will then link directly to your feed. But don't do this just yet.

076 Preview and validate

Before you start to publicize your feed, you should first ensure that it is valid. To do this simply select the Validate link, which in turn will add your feed to http://feedvalidator.org, and inform you whether your feed is valid. Finally, you can select XML to see how your feed will look in Firefox, Bloglines, or other readers.

077 Publish your feed

Once you're happy with your feed, you can place the necessary code on your site. Now when users visit your site and see this link, they will be able to add it to their reader of choice.

del.icio.us

It's easy to take links for granted, but they are the building blocks of the web, and as such are worth managing in the best possible way. Despite Firefox being a brilliant browser and having decent bookmark support, it doesn't store links online. What this means is that you can't universally access your links using Firefox alone, and with many of us using multiple machines this can be a real pain. This is why in 2003 Joshua Schachter created the web-based bookmarking site del.icio.us (http://del.icio.us), and in doing so became one of Web 2.0's premier poster boys. del.icio.us enables millions of web users to access and manage their bookmarks like never before. We're going to show you how to get started with del.icio.us, and we'll even provide you with some fantastic power user tips so you can get even more from the service!

078 Get registered

First up, visit http://del.icio.us and register (you'll find the Register link at the top right of the home page). First select a username. This will show up if you make your links public, so keep it clean and simple.

080 It's all blank!

Select the Your Bookmarks link at the top left of the page, and you'll see, well, not a lot. Thankfully, del.icio.us doesn't bombard you with irrelevant information, so until you start adding some links, you're going to have a pretty sparse page before you.

079 Install the browser buttons

Next, you'll be asked if you'd like to install del.icio.us buttons in your browser–this is a good idea, so select Install Extension Now. You'll have to restart your browser before these buttons appear in your interface. Finally, a verification email is sent to you, so you'll need to access your email account to confirm your registration.

081 Activate privacy

Before you start adding links, it's worth noting that by default the links you add will be public. We recommend enabling the option to save links privately. To do this you must enter the Settings section, and select Private Settings. On the next page is a check box; highlight it, and select Change Settings. Now whenever you add a new bookmark, a Do Not Share option will be available.

082 Adding a site

Adding new links is a cinch. To add a site that you're currently visiting, all you need to do is hit the TAG button at the top of your browser, and a new window will open. Here you can make notes, set the privacy of your bookmark, and add tags.

083 Adding a link

If there's a link present on a page that you'd like to add to del.icio.us, then all you need to do is hover over the link, right-click your mouse, and scroll to Bookmark This Link In del.icio.us.

084 Adding tags

del.icio.us is all about the tagging! Tags are single words that help you manage and maintain your bookmarks. Get in the habit of writing about five tags for each link, and remember that you can only use single words, so if a tag has more than one word you should separate them with hyphens.

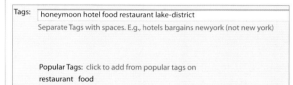

085 Suggested tags

del.icio.us is a social bookmarking site, which means that when you make a link public, you help contribute to the del.icio.us community. This means that if others have already bookmarked a page, then there will already be Popular tags to choose from (just click them and they'll be added). And as you add more tags, del.icio.us will start to recommend existing tags, too.

Recommended Tags: click to add from your existing tags
bird birds camera nature photography

Popular Tags: click to add from popular tags on
birding birds forum nature photography bird ornithology wildlife

086 Fill her up!

If you haven't already, try adding some more bookmarks to del.icio.us ... You done? Good. Now you've got some favorites saved in your account, you can get a better feel for the del.icio.us interface. Along the top you have links to your sections of the site (as well as settings), in the main window are your bookmarks, and on the right you can see a list of the tags that you've attributed to your bookmarks.

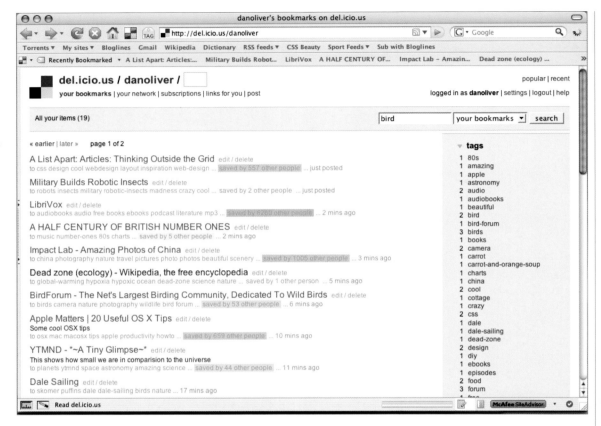

087 Search your bookmarks

Now we're going to show you a few cool features that you can access via the del.icio.us site, and the first of these is the Search option. Available at the top right of the site, the Search field enables you to search within your bookmarks, within del.icio.us, and across the web. This search includes all the words within each link, including tags.

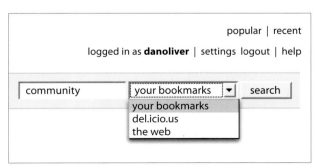

088 Tag search

At the very top of the del.icio.us page you'll see your URL with an area where you can enter text. In this box you can place any tag (with multiples separated by a + sign), and have them returned by del.icio.us. This is why tagging is so cool.

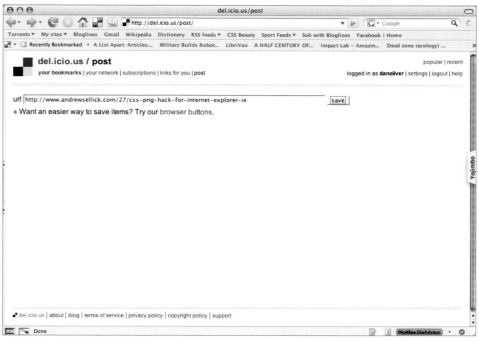

089 Spread your tags

When you place tags on the end of your URL, you can then distribute this link and anyone—not just you—will be able to view your tagged links.

090 The old school approach

OK, so you're not always going to be accessing del.icio.us via a machine that has the del.icio.us add-on installed, so you still need to know how to add a URL manually. It's a bit clunky–given how easy it is with the del.icio.us add-on–but you'll need to copy the URL you want to add, select the Post link at the top of del.icio.us, paste the link, hit save, and add the relevant details.

del.icio.us: take things further

Now we've introduced the basics of del.icio.us, it's time to check out some of the cooler "hidden" features on offer, as well as checking out some tweaks that will improve your del.icio.us experience even further.

091 Subscriptions

The Subscriptions section is the hidden gem within del.icio.us—but not anymore! This section used to be called Inbox, and it enables you to subscribe to various tags and see new sites that include these tags as they're added to del.icio.us (another example of the social aspect of the site). To add a new Subscription just click the Subscriptions link at the top of the site, and this will take you to a page where you can add a tag to subscribe to, and even specify a user (leave this field blank if you want to see all additions with this tag).

People: subscriptions

This is where you set up your tag subscriptions, which allow you to keep track of all new bookmarks saved with tags that interest you. View your subscriptions page at del.icio.us/subscriptions/danoliver.

subscribe to a tag
tag   monkeys
only from this user [ ]   (leave blank for all)
    subscribe

label subscription

092 Mix your tabs

To refine your subscriptions, you can just add a + sign in between your tags. Now, to access your Subscriptions you just need to select the Subscriptions link, and either view all the new links, or choose specific subscriptions from the menu on the right.

your subs
*/british+wildlife X
*/manchester+united X
*/monkeys X
*/motogp X
*/nascar X
*/photography+nature X

» edit

093 Monitor other users

You may start to see the same users cropping up in your Subscriptions, so why not see all their subscriptions, too! Just type http://del.icio.us/subscriptions/username, and replace username with the user you want to check out. You'll then be able to see all their Subscriptions.

094 Popular/ recent

Sometimes it's fun to browse the popular and recent links being added to del.icio.us. You can do this by—surprise, surprise—selecting the Popular or Recent link from the top right of your del.icio.us page.

095 Tag for friends

This option enables you to share links with other del.icio.us users. If you come across a link that may be of interest to another user, just add the tag "for:USERNAME," and the link will show up in the Links For You section of del.icio.us.

096 Feed me now!

Now that you're familiar with feeds, you'll appreciate what a great addition they are to del.icio.us. Using feeds, you can keep up-to-date with various tags. For individual tags add the following link:
http://del.icio.us/rss/tag/TAGNAME
For combined tags use this link:
http://del.icio.us/rss/tag/TAGNAME+TAGNAME

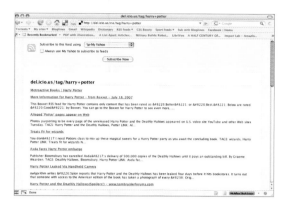

097 Take feeds further

You can even use feeds to keep updated with individual users on del.icio.us. To do this, just use the following link: http://del.icio.us/rss/USERNAME, or, to keep up with subscriptions, use: http://del.icio.us/rss/subscriptions/USERNAME.

098 Add del.icio.us links to your site

Go into Settings, and under Blogging, click on a link called Link Rolls. This will provide you with a chunk of code and some settings you can edit (these include whether to display an icon, a title for the roll, etc.). As you change settings, the code will update on the fly, and when you're done you can copy that code and place it in your site or blog code.

099 Create a tag cloud

There are certain page elements that have become synonymous with Web 2.0, and the tag cloud is one of them. A tag cloud is a collection of words with those mentioned most often given more prominence in the cloud. For instance, if most of your links are tagged with "monkey," then "monkey" will dominate your tag cloud. Go to Settings, look under Blogging, and select Tag Rolls. Now you can edit the settings and have the code generated for your site.

100 Add me to your network

To grow your del.icio.us network, you can place a badge on your site. Again, click in the Settings, look under Blogging, and select Network Badges. Here you can choose whether a logo displays and how visitors will see your name. At the bottom of the page is some JavaScript, which simply needs adding to your site or blog.

103 delicious_blank

delicious_blank is a Greasemonkey script for Firefox (see tip 040), and it enables you to have del.icio.us links open in a new tab. To install the script go to http://userscripts.org/scripts/show/3193, and select the Install This Script link on the right. You can manage scripts by going to Tools>Greasemonkey in the Firefox menu.

104 Use Spotlight to search del.icio.us

Unfortunately, this tip is for Mac users only. If you use a version of Mac OS with Spotlight, then, by installing Delimport (which is free), you can search URL, title, description, and tags within Spotlight. Install Delimport at ianhenderson.org/delimport.html

101 Export your Firefox bookmarks

If you've already spent a long time adding bookmarks to Firefox, do not despair. You can easily import all your existing Firefox bookmarks to del.icio.us, but first you'll have to export them. Go to Bookmarks>Organize Bookmarks in Firefox, and when the Bookmarks manager opens go to File>Export. Save the file to your Desktop.

102 Import to Firefox

Now you've exported your Firefox links, you can add them to del.icio.us. Select Settings, and under Bookmarks click on the Import/Upload link. Hit the Browse button, and navigate to the Firefox file you've just saved. Once you're happy with the import settings, hit Import Now at the bottom of the page.

105 Search via Firefox

When you install the Firefox add-on, two main buttons appear in your browser. We've already covered the Tag button, but what does the one next to it do? Well, it lets you search, of course! Select the del.icio.us logo, and a search drop-down appears. You can either type a search term here, or you can select the little blue arrow, which will open del.icio.us in your sidebar (if you installed the All-in-One Sidebar).

107 Daily blog posting

Is your blog powered by WordPress, Typepad, or Movable Type? Do you want to automatically let visitors to your blog know about the links you add each day? If the answer to these questions is "yes," then there's an experimental del.icio.us feature that's perfect for you. Under Blogging in the Settings section, you'll find a category called Daily Blog Posting. You'll need a few details to hand, such as your blog username, your password, the full URL of the XML-RPC interface for your blog (the file should be called xmlrpc.php), and your blog ID number (which is probably 1, but should be left blank for WordPress users). As an added extra, you can even set which category these posts will be filed under (you'll need a category ID for this, which can be found within your blog's settings). Now add these details, and wait for the magic to happen!

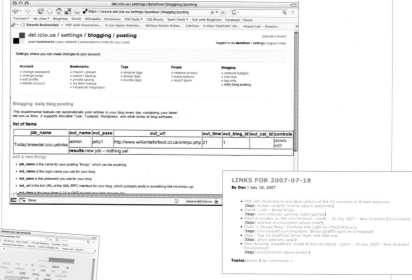

106 Pretty things

Let's face it, links ain't pretty, but they are when you run them through Revealicious (www.ivy.fr/revealicious). Go to the site, sign in with your del.icio.us details, and have your links presented in visual splendor. It's interactive, it's built in Flash, and it's a site well worth visiting.

Blogger

Blogger is the best platform for newcomers to the world of blogging (there are more powerful platforms—such as WordPress and Movable Type—but they require more technical know-how). But first, we should take a step back. What is a blog? Put simply, a blog is a site that enables you to easily manage information that you wish to add to a site in chronological format. This could be a personal diary, a political soapbox, a reviews site, or anything else that can be presented via chronological posting. Blogs are made up of posts, which can include text, images, audio, and video; they also have an interactive element, which enables visitors to comment on posts. In this chapter we'll show you how to set up your own blog, create a template, manage comments, archive posts, manage feeds, incorporate adverts, blog from your cellphone, and much more besides.

Blogger basics

108 Get started

First, you need to visit www.blogger.com. On the homepage select the Create Your Own Blog button. If you already have a Google Gmail account, the next screen will display your details (so long as you haven't cleared out your cookies recently). The reason for this, if you haven't already guessed, is that this is yet another Google-owned company.

109 Add a display name

On this first sign-up page you'll be asked for a display name, which will be used when you post a new blog entry, so make sure it isn't a name you'll be embarrassed about publishing to the world.

110 Name and address, please

On the next screen you must create a blog title and blog address (the URL of your finished blog). The title can be anything you like, but your desired address may already be taken by someone else, so try to be inventive.

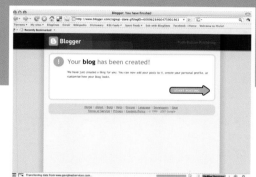

111 Advanced Blog Setup

Blogger has two hosting options. You can either host your blog on Blogspot (Blogger's free hosting platform) or—if you have your own webspace and domain name—you can use Advanced Blog Setup. For now we're going to use Blogspot.

112 Choose a template

There's plenty you can do to modify the look of your blog once you've set it up, but for now you need to choose one of the available Blogger templates. Once you're done, select continue.

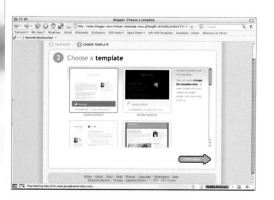

113 That's it!

Your blog has now been created. How simple was that? But we're not finished yet. All we've done is secure our place on the Blogspot network, and now we can start to have some fun with our new blog. Next, select Start Posting.

114 The Posting section

You should now be taken to the Posting section within Blogger. Here you'll see two entry fields; the top one is where you enter the title of any new post, and the main one is where you put the content. Above this field you'll see a series of buttons, which enable you to style your post.

115 Write a test post

Blogger's powerful text editor enables you to choose from a selection of fonts, style up your text, choose different colors, insert links, add pictures, spell-check your posts, and more! Write a test post, and get acquainted with the different tools.

THE HENLEY COLLEGE LIBRARY

116 Autosave

Before we publish our first post, there are a few other options to highlight. First up, Blogger has a brilliant Autosave function. There's nothing worse than losing a well-crafted blog post, and by saving every minute Blogger ensures this never happens. Wait one minute, and you'll see a Draft Autosaved message below your post. Reassuring.

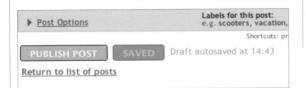

117 Post Options

By default, all your posts will be enabled for comments so that visitors to your blog can discuss your posts; however, if you wish to change this then select Post Options under the main entry window, and select Do Not Allow. Finally, select Preview to the top right of your entry, and, if everything's good-to-go, select Publish Post.

118 The next step

Visit your new blog, and your post will be displayed in all its glory. But you've probably already got some questions. Why is the time under my post wrong (as it invariably is)? Why are my details blank? What's that bar at the top of my blog? What's that Customize link for? In the next few pages we'll answer all these questions.

119 The Blogger home page

Whenever you want to make changes to your blog, simply enter via www.blogger.com. Your blog shows at the top of the page, and any new blog you create within this account will appear below it.

122 Add a picture to your profile

If you already have a photo online, simply paste its location into the Photo URL box in the details section. If you don't have a picture online, you can put one in a Blogger post, and use the resulting URL. Alternatively, you can use a free hosting service such as www.allyoucanupload.com. (Optimize images for the web before uploading.)

123 Add a description

If the title of your blog requires a little explanation, then you can add a description of up to 500 characters, which will then sit under your title. To change this go to the Settings tab, and add your text to the Description box.

120 Got the time?

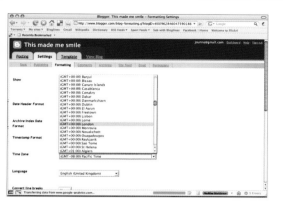

Select settings from your main page, and you'll jump to the Settings tab. In this section are a series of subsections; select Formatting. Here you can set how many posts display on the main page, but—more importantly—you can also set your local time under Time Zone.

121 Add some details

To get a decent profile on your blog, head back to your Dashboard (this link always appears at the top of the page within Blogger). Select Edit Profile on the right, and specify what information you would like to appear on your blog. Don't provide your date of birth or any other personal information that you wouldn't want to fall into the wrong hands.

124 Adding an image to a post

Now we'll add an image to a post. Under the Posting tab, select Create. Hit the Add Image tab, and a new window opens. Now navigate to an image on your hard drive or online, choose a layout option, and select an image size. Images will display as small, medium, or large on your blog, but when you click on the image it will take you to the original file you uploaded (so don't upload high-res photos, unless you want your visitors to be able to access them).

125 Add meta data

Blogger is owned by Google, so your blog should appear in its listings fairly quickly; however, you should still add meta data to your blog (bits of code that tell search engines about your site). For this we need to get under the hood. Go to the Template section, select Edit HTML from the submenu, and add the following code directly below the <head> tag:

<meta content='ADD YOUR SITE DESCRIPTION HERE' name='description'/>
<meta content='ADD YOUR KEYWORDS HERE – COMMA SEPARATED' name='keywords'/>
<meta content='ADD YOUR NAME HERE' name='author'/>

126 The blue bar

By using Blogger's free hosting, you agree to have the blue bar appear at the top of your blog. It's a small price to pay for free hosting, and if you want to remove it then you'll have to host the blog on your own space.

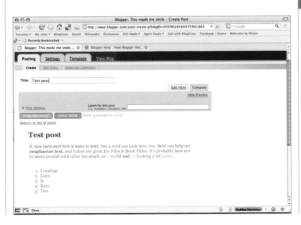

127 Comments

Comments are an important part of any blog. In the Comments section, under the Settings tab, you have three choices of who can post to your blog (anyone, registered Blogger or Google users, or people who you've given permission to post). Possibly the most useful option in this section though, is the ability to ask those commenting to provide word verification before they do so, thus avoiding comment spam. We suggest changing this setting to Yes straightaway.

128 Comment notification

When people post comments on your blog, they'll often be asking you questions. To make sure you're notified as soon as new comments appear, you can provide an email address, to which new comment notifications will be sent.

129 Archiving

Depending on how frequently you plan to post, you can set different archiving intervals under Archiving in the Settings section. If you don't plan on posting too often then choose Monthly; if you're going to post like a mad thing, choose Daily.

130 Post Pages

In the Archiving section there's an important option called Enable Post Pages?, which should be set to Yes; then each of your posts will have a unique URL created for it. This makes it easy to share your posts with others, improves your blog's accessibility, and also improves your chance of better search rankings (your links will have a logical format, such as http://yourblog.blogspot.com/year/month/title-of-post.html).

131 Blog Feeds

Having already covered feeds in the first chapter, hopefully you can now appreciate how useful they can be. Under Site Feed in the Settings section, there are a few options to choose between. First—next to Allow Blog Feed—select whether you want no feed, a feed that displays the first paragraph of each post, or one that displays your entire post to subscribers.

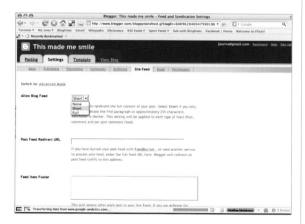

132 Advanced Feeds

Once you've decided on a feed, enter the Advanced Mode. In this section you can choose individual settings for blog posts, blog comments, and per post comments; thus giving you control over exactly which areas of your blog people can get feeds for.

133 Blog to mail

In the Settings section you'll find a subsection called Email. Select Email, and you'll see two text fields. The first field enables you to have each post you add to your blog emailed to an address of your choice.

134 Mail to blog

Now we'll look at how you can email posts to your blog. First you will need to set a Mail-to-Blogger Address (keep this secret, as anyone with this address will be able to post to your blog), and make sure the Publish option is selected. Now, any email sent to the address you've just specified will be posted to your blog. You can't post images or attachments, your email subject will become the post's title, and you'll need to put "#end" before any information—such as signatures—that you don't want added to the post.

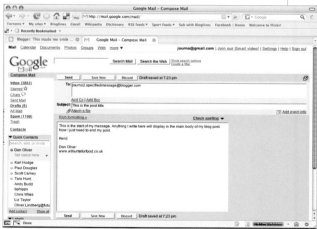

Page Elements

135 Page Elements

Under the Template tag, the first link you'll notice is Page Elements. This enables you to add and edit blog components. There's so much you can do in this section, and over the next four pages, we'll reveal how you can personalize your blog to the max! To get started, select Page Elements, and you'll see outlines of your various blog elements.

136 Edit Elements

Existing Page Elements can be changed by selecting the relevant Edit link. A new window will open, and you'll be able to edit things such as information hierarchy and what displays on your blog.

137 Move Elements

Thanks to the talented developers at Blogger, you can actually drag and drop Elements to where you wish them to appear on your blog. If you want your About Me section to appear first, simply select it, and drag the element to the top of the page.

138 Header image

To give your blog a bit more personality, add your own header image. Using the MeasureIt add-on in Firefox, measure the dimensions of the current blog header. Now create a new header using these dimensions. Select the Edit link in your header, and a new window will open. Browse to your new banner on your hard drive, and select Save Changes. If the banner doesn't replace the original but sits behind it, go back into the edit section, and choose Instead of Title and Description.

139 Edit Blog Posts

The last section we'll cover while discussing editing is Blog Posts. Select the Edit link, and a new window will open. In this window you can select how your blog posts will be formatted, with the option to turn off elements such as who an entry was posted by, what labels were attributed to it, and when it was posted. You can even change some of your blog terminology, such as changing Comments to Wibbles–or something.

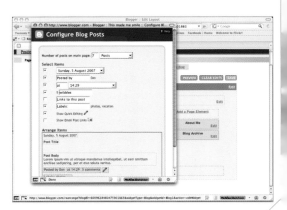

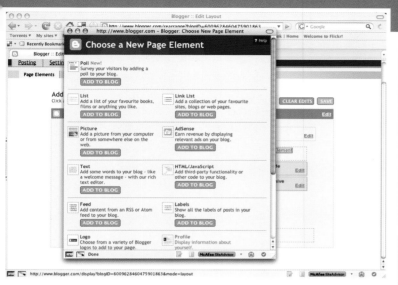

142 Add a list

Everyone loves a good list, especially those of us with mild OCD. If you'd like to add a list of your favorite movies, books, meals, or whatever, then add the List element to your blog. In the setup page, you can give your list a title, select how it displays, and add new list items.

143 Poll your visitors

New elements are being added to Blogger all the time, and one of the newest is the ability to add a poll to your blog. Once you've selected Add to Blog, you'll see a number of poll options. You'll need to specify a question, and then provide a series of possible answers that visitors can select. Lastly, choose the closing date and time of your poll.

140 Add a Page Element

Now we're going to look at some of the new elements you can add to your blog. Select the Add a Page Element link, and a new window will open, with 15 new additions to choose from. In the next few pages we'll look at the best.

141 Add an image

Many bloggers like to add images to their sidebar, and Blogger has addressed this requirement. Select the Add a Page Element link, and select the Add to Blog button in the Picture section. A new window opens, and you can navigate to your image of choice. Select Shrink to Fit, and the image will fit perfectly into your sidebar.

144 Add text

It's not the sexiest of Page Elements, but sometimes you just want to add a bit of text to your blog—this is particularly useful for welcome messages. Select Add a Page Element, choose Text, and add a title and body text (you can style it using the WYSIWYG editor). Now go back to the Page Elements, and drag the text to the desired position.

145 Add HTML/JavaScript

Thankfully, the guys behind Blogger aren't averse to you adding code that pulls content from other websites, via the APIs (application programming interface) of those sites and web apps. We'll look at the Flickr API in the next chapter and reveal the code you need to have your Flickr photos appear automatically on your blog using the HTML/JavaScript element (see tips 208-211). If you already have code you'd like to add, select HTML/JavaScript from the selection of Page Elements and paste it into the main text area.

147 Remember to save

This may seem like an obvious thing to point out, but you should always remember to save changes to your page layout as you go along, or you could get a shock when you next visit your blog.

146 List your links

Using the Link List element you can create your very own blogrolls. As with all the Page Elements, you can create multiple instances, and using Link List you can highlight your favorite sites, add links to friends' pages, or even links to multimedia content. The formatting is the same as the Links element, but with the addition of a URL field for each list item.

148 Remember: think hierarchy

At this point you may well be throwing everything at your blog, so think about its hierarchy. Put yourself in the position of someone visiting your blog for the first time, and then you'll realize that maybe putting a poll at the top of your page isn't the best idea. Just remember there are usually two things you must address before any other content on a blog: who you are and what your blog's about.

149 Video Bar

As part of the "Google Gang," you have a wealth of content at your fingertips, including Google and YouTube videos. Add the Video Bar element to your site, and a selection of four videos will display in a bar—horizontally or vertically—on your blog. You can specify what videos appear by using comma-separated search terms.

150 Add a feed

We've already covered feeds in some detail in the first chapter, and Blogger enables you to place new feeds on your blog via the Page Element called, not surprisingly, Feed. Select Add to Blog under the Feed heading, then paste your feed URL into the address bar. Lastly, in the next screen you can edit your title, and choose how many items display.

151 Label stuff

The Labels element enables you to highlight the labels that you've attributed to each post. This is a nice way to show what you post most frequently about, and you can have them sorted alphabetically or via frequency.

152 Getting rid of elements

Despite the benefits of Page Elements, adding too many can make your blog look messy. Thankfully, removing them is simple. Just select the Edit link next to an element, and choose Remove Page Element.

153 Go logo!

If you'd like to advertise that your blog is from the Blogger stable, you can choose a Page Element called Logo, which will insert a logo in your blog.

154 It makes AdSense

With this tip, we've saved the best til last. You probably won't become the next Donald Trump with AdSense, but it's a nice way of getting a bit of extra money. Using AdSense, Google will place adverts on your site based on the contents of your blog. Once you've chosen the AdSense element, you'll be prompted to create a new account. Having done this, you'll then be able to choose the color and dimension of your advert. That's it! Now you can move the ad to the best place on your blog (make sure it's visible when visitors enter your site).

Tweaking the design

155 Modify your blog

Thus far we've done a minimal amount of tweaking to the look of our blog, but this doesn't have to be the case. Blogger has some great editing options within the Template section, and in the next couple of pages we'll show you how to give your blog a personal touch.

156 Fonts and Colors

Within the Templates section, select Fonts and Colors. To the left you'll see a scrollable window featuring the different elements of your site. As you select each element in this window, the rest of the information to the right will change accordingly.

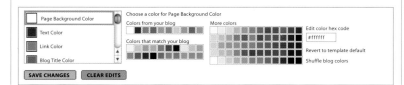

157 Previewing changes

When you're in the Fonts and Colors section, you'll notice that you have a split screen. Whenever you make a change to any of your blog's characteristics, they will change instantly, and you'll be able to get a live preview in the bottom half of your browser window. At any point you can select Revert to Template Default, and your blog will return to its original state.

158 Pop-out

Having your editing options and preview window in the same screen can seriously limit the amount of screen estate you have. To have more of your blog displaying as you make changes, you can select the Pop-out link, to the right of the editing area. This will open a new window that features your editing options, and show more of your blog in the main browser window.

159 Complementary colors

As you change the colors on your blog, Blogger automatically suggests a selection of complementary colors in the Colors that Match your Blog section. This is a very useful tool, especially if you're struggling with schemes for your blog.

160 Use a single color

If you'd like to base your blog's color scheme on one particular color, then here's what to do. First, go through all the sections of your site and set them to white by highlighting them and then selecting white from the More Colors box. Then select the single color that you want to use as your base in the More Colors box (this obviously works for multiple colors, too).

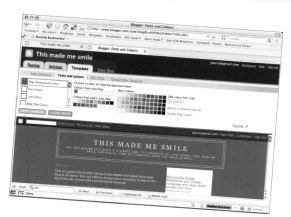

161 Shuffle colors

If you have a set of colors that you like, but can't think of where you want to use them, then you can use the Shuffle Blog Colors link. Just keep selecting the Shuffle Blog Colors link, and your chosen colors will be applied to different elements.

Edit color hex code

#ffffff

Revert to template default

Shuffle blog colors

162 Fontastic!

As well as changing color, you can also change the font attributes for sections of your blog. Scroll down to a font in the scrollable area to the left, select it, and then choose how you want the font to be displayed (you can change font, set the size, and choose between normal, italic, and bold).

163 Change your template

OK, if changing your blog's color scheme hasn't got rid of the urge for change, then it's time for drastic measures. Under the Template heading select Choose New Template, and you'll see a host of different templates. There are 16 to choose from, with some having up to four different schemes in the set. Once you've found a template you like the look of, you can select Preview to have your existing blog content displayed in the new format. Once you're happy, select the template you want, and hit the orange Save Template button.

164 Edit HTML

Blogger has plenty of ways of editing your blog without touching the HTML, but if there's something you really want to change, you can do so. Select Edit HTML in the Template section, and select the Download Full Template link before you do anything else. This will save your current blog. Now, you can make changes to your site's HTML in the Edit Template window.

Get noticed

You could have the best-looking blog on the web, but unless it adheres to a few promotion principles, you're going to miss out on a big chunk of traffic. Here, we'll provide some of the best ways to maximize your marketing potential, and introduce you to Google Analytics; after all, if you don't know how many visitors you have, how can you monitor how well your site's performing?

165 Google Analytics

In the next few steps we're going to introduce you to one of Google's most vaunted applications: Google Analytics. Google Analytics enables you to monitor and analyze your site traffic, and it's totally free. If you don't have an account, go to www.google.com/analytics and sign up.

166 Add Website Profile

Once you've signed up, select Add Website Profile. Provide your blog's URL, and on the next page you'll be presented with a page titled Tracking Status, which includes a block of code; copy the code, and select Done.

167 Place the code

Go back to the Page Elements section in Blogger and select Add a Page Element in the footer of your page (you must select the link in the footer). Choose HTML/JavaScript, and paste the code into the field (leaving the title blank). Now, head back to your Google Analytics home page, click the Check Status link, and wait as Google gathers your site information. This can take a while, but don't get impatient.

168 Think about titles

The titles of your blog posts need to meet two criteria. Firstly, they need to appeal to your target audience. Keep titles punchy, relevant, and in keeping with your blog's tone. Secondly, they need to appeal to search engines. Enter one of your titles at http://inventory.overture.com, and you'll get an idea of what people are searching for on Yahoo. If you can meet both these criteria, you'll be well on the way to title success.

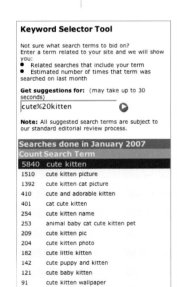

169 Hide your obscurity

Rome wasn't built in a day, and–although your blog was–this doesn't mean you're going to have an amphitheater of visitors, hungry for your next soliloquy. With this in mind, it may be prudent to turn off comments on your blog until you start getting more than a handful of visitors each day. To do this go to the Settings section, select Comments from the submenu, and opt to Hide comments.

170 Email posts

While you're still in the Settings section, select Basic from the submenu. In this section you'll see the option to Show Email Post Links, change this to Yes. Now, a small envelope will appear under each post, and when a visitor selects this, they'll be able to email any post to a friend. Great promotion, and best of all it's free!

171 Add to listings

In the Basic submenu, you'll also see the option to Add Your Blog To Our Listings. You should ensure this is set to Yes. Next, go to Publishing in the submenu, and set Send Pings to Yes (this will notify various sites when your blog is updated).

172 Stay regular

This might seem like stating the obvious–and it is–but this is one of the best pieces of advice we can give when it comes to blogging: write posts often. This, more than anything else, will keep visitors coming back to your blog, and will also enable you to hone your writing style.

173 Get Feedburner

Feeds are vital for your blog. The people that subscribe to your feed are your lifeblood. To monitor those subscribing to your feed you can use FeedBurner (www.feedburner.com). This is another company Google has acquired, so once you've set up your FeedBurner account, you can post your feed in the Post Feed Redirect URL box in your Blogger settings (in the Site Feed submenu under Settings). Blogger will now redirect all post feed traffic to this new address.

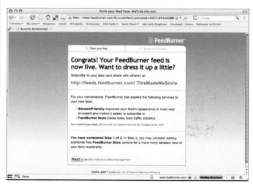

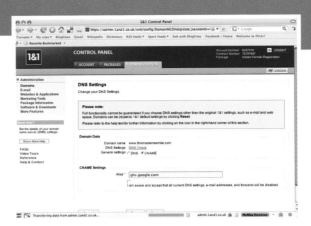

Blogger: take things further

Hopefully, by now you've got a good feel for the Blogger platform and understand just how powerful it is. Next we'll show you how to get even more from your blog, including instructions on how to get your very own domain name!

174 Beyond Blogspot

There may come a point when you want to get your own URL for your blog, and this is a relatively simple procedure. The first thing you need to do is find a domain name (we were lucky, and found that www.thismademesmile.com was available!). Although you can also host your blog away from Blogger, at this stage we're just going to show you how to publish a custom domain.

175 CNAME record

This is probably the trickiest stage of the process. Once you've purchased your domain, you'll need to provide details that will connect your new domain with your existing blog. To do this you will need to create a CNAME record for your domain, and associate it with ghs.google.com. You can get extensive directions for a number of registrars by going to http://help.blogger.com, and typing CNAME into the search window on the right. Once you've done this, it may take a few days for this information to be communicated to every server on the net. Be patient.

176 But that's not my domain

The more eagle-eyed among you will have noticed that we just instructed you to point your domain to ghs.google.com, which seems pretty generic—that's because it is. DNS (domain name system) servers now know to point your URL at Google, but that's it. Now we need to provide a bit more information, which will direct traffic to your blog. Go to Settings in Blogger, and select the Publishing submenu. Now choose the Custom Domain link, and insert your domain in the Your Domain box.

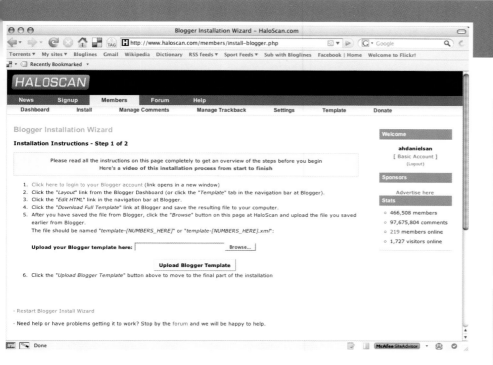

179 Blogger Mobile

There's no doubt that blogging from your cellphone is cool, but it's only available on certain networks. If you're lucky enough to be with one of these providers, just send a message from your phone–which can include a photo–to go@blogger.com, and a new blog will automatically be produced that features this post.

180 I don't need a new blog!

Creating a completely new blog isn't much good if you already have one that you want to update. But help is at hand. Once you've made your first post you'll be sent a voucher, and you will then be able to add this voucher to http://go.blogger.com (this is called "claiming your blog"). Once you've claimed your blog you can switch to your existing blog, and all subsequent mobile posts will be added to it.

177 TrackBack: part one

Now we'll look at some of the hottest tools for Blogger, and first up is HaloScan (http://haloscan.com). HaloScan facilitates the use of TrackBack on Blogger. If you haven't heard of it before, TrackBack is a way for you to comment on someone else's blog, but from your own site. You then inform the owner of that blog that you've commented on their post, and the circle is complete (for more information visit Wikipedia at http://en.wikipedia.org/wiki/Trackback).

178 TrackBack: part two

To add TrackBack, go to the HaloScan site and register. Once you've done this you'll see the Blogger Installation Wizard. You'll have to go to Blogger and save a copy of your template, upload this to HaloScan, and then upload the new template–generated by HaloScan–back to Blogger (comments will have to be enabled to see the new TrackBack link).

181 Scribefire and Blogger

We've already touched on ScribeFire, and how it enables you to easily make blog posts from within Firefox (see tip 032). To enable ScribeFire for Blogger, press F8 in Firefox, select the Add button to the right, insert your URL, then provide your username and password.

183 Periodical pinging

There are lots of blogging services out there, and pinging them lets them know that your site has been updated. To do this simply pop along to Pingoat: here you can enter your blog name, the URL for your site, and then choose from a host of sites you'd like to ping.

184 Recent comments

If you're using a Classic Blogger template, you can make some neat changes to your template. One such change is the ability to have recent posts display on your blog. To do this you need to place the following code in your blog, where you want the comments to appear:

```
<MainPage>
<h2 class="sidebar-title">Recent Comments</h2>
<ul>
<Blogger>
<BlogItemCommentsEnabled>
<BlogItemComments>
<li><$BlogCommentAuthor$> //
<a href="<$BlogCommentPermalinkURL$>">
<$BlogCommentDateTime$></a></li>
</BlogItemComments>
</BlogItemCommentsEnabled>
</Blogger>
</ul>
</MainPage>
```

182 Creative Commons

As standard, your blog has no copyright info. To remedy this, go to http://creativecommons.org, select License Your Work, choose your license details, hit the Select a License button, choose a logo, and copy the resulting text into a new HTML/JavaScript Page Element. Now place this element in the footer of your blog.

185 Here comes the Favicon

Ever visited a site and seen a small image in the address bar or tab, or bookmarked a site and had an image appear in your favorites? Well, that's a Favicon. In the next couple of steps we're going to show you how to create your own and apply it to your blog.

`http://www.blogger.com/home`

186 Create your Favicon

In your image-editing package of choice, create a 16 x 16 pixel image. Having done this, you'll notice something: it's tiny! Because of this, you need to think about what your icon should be (we'd suggest passing on anything too intricate). Once you've saved your image (as a JPEG or GIF), go to www.html-kit.com/favicon/, find your image on your hard drive, and select Generate Favicon.ico. Finally, select Download Favicon.

187 Upload your Favicon

You will now have a .ico file (which will show up in Internet Explorer), and a PNG file in a folder called Extra within the unzipped folder you've just downloaded, which will display in browsers that don't support .ico. Now you need to upload your .ico and PNG files to some webspace. If you don't have hosting, you won't be able to use most free image hosts, as the .ico file format won't be supported. However, you can sign up for free hosting with a service such as Tripod (www.tripod.lycos.com), and host your .ico and PNG files there.

188 Display your Favicon

In the Layout section, go to Template and select the Edit HTML submenu. Now, insert the following code in between the <head></head> tags, and above the <title></title> tags, on your blog: **<link href='http://yoururl.com/favicon.ico' rel='shortcut icon' type='image/x-icon'/>**
<link href='http://youurl.com/favicon.png' rel='icon' type='image/png'/>
Now the Blogger Favicon should be overridden, and yours will be displayed in all its miniature glory.

Flickr

There are two words that sum Flickr up: photo phenomenon. Flickr has a host of brilliant features, but the simple way to describe it is as a photo-sharing website and community. In this chapter you'll discover how to get started with Flickr, the best ways to manage your photos, some of the cool ways you can use Flickr on other sites, and how a Pro account differs from the vanilla standard.

Flickr basics

189 Create an account

To sign up, you need to go to www.flickr.com and select the Create Your Account button. At this point you'll notice something strange; that's right, Google doesn't actually own Flickr, Yahoo! does. If you already have a Yahoo! ID, you can use that to sign in. Alternatively, hit the Sign Up link. Once you've entered your details, choose Create A New Account.

190 Flickr home

The next page may look a little daunting, so we'll quickly go through the different sections. You navigate Flickr by using the links at the top of each page, and the main ones we'll be concentrating on are You, Organize, Contacts, and Groups. You'll also see a small envelope at the top right, which is where new messages will appear, and where you go to send messages.

191 Profile page

Although you're probably desperate to get some photos online, there's a bit of housekeeping to do first. Select the You link, scroll down to Your Profile, and you'll be taken to the Personal Information page. Here you can tell people about yourself, set privacy levels, and add a "buddy icon," an image which will be displayed across the Flickr universe.

192 Buddy Icon

Select Edit in the Your Buddy Icon section, and the next screen will provide you with an upload option on the right. The Buddy Icon displays at 48 x 48 pixels, and you can create your own image at these dimensions and just select Upload. If you don't have the necessary software, though, Flickr has provided an Icon Builder.

193 Icon Builder

To use the Icon Builder, first select where your start image resides (in your Flickr photos, on your computer, or on the web). Once you've done this, a browse box will appear, and you should navigate to your image (there's a limit of 2MB on file sizes). Your image now displays, and you can drag a box over your desired area; if you want to fit more of the image in, drag a corner of the bounding box. You'll see a preview in the top left, and once you're done, hit Make The Icon.

194 Simple uploads

Right, now it's time to upload some pictures. Go to You in the menu (remembering to select the little triangle next to the main link), and scroll down to Upload Pictures. Next, select the Choose Photos link and a new window will open, enabling you to browse your hard drive. Now select the images you'd like to upload.

195 Set privacy

Now the images you selected will display in Flickr, with a series of options available under a Set Privacy heading. For now, select Public (we'll look at private settings later), and select Upload Photos. You'll now be able to monitor the upload progress of your images.

196 Describe photos

Next up, you'll be asked to describe your photos. By default, the titles of your images will remain the same as they were when you uploaded them, but you can change them at this point to make the titles more relevant. Under the title, you can also add a more detailed description of the image.

197 Add tags

Tags enable you to find and organize your photos with ease. At the top of the current screen you'll see the option to Batch tag your images–applying the same tags to all photos–or you can tag them individually. Separate tags with commas, and if you have a tag that's more than one word, put it in quote marks.

Get organized

198 What's a set?

Here, we'll show you how to use the Organize section and create your first set. A set is a way of grouping your images, so you can easily manage and publish them to the wider world. To get organized, select the main Organize link at the top of Flickr. This will open a new interface.

199 The interface

As you can see, the Organize section of Flickr looks fantastic, and—as you'll learn—it's also intuitive and easy to use. Your images are displayed along the bottom of the interface, and you can scroll through them using the arrows at the far left and right. To edit images, you simply drag them into the main area.

200 Make further changes

At any point, you can enter the Organize section and update the information linked to your images. Just drag an image into the main window—it doesn't matter which tab you're in—and then double-click the image. The details of that image will then display, and you can edit tags, titles, dates, permissions, and more.

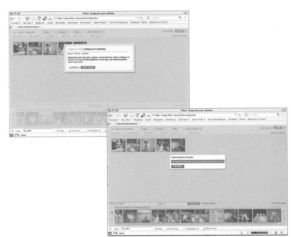

201 Batch Organize

The first tab in the Organize section enables you to change the settings for multiple images, and is labeled Batch Organize. Drag all the images that you'd like to make changes to into the main window, then select the attribute that you'd like to amend from the Batch Organize submenu.

202 Sets education

First, select the Sets tab at the top of the interface. As soon as you drag a photo onto the main window, a number of new options appear. You can now enter the name of your new set, provide a description, and edit and arrange your photos. When you're happy with your set, select Save. (The free account only supports three sets.)

203 Showing sets

Go back to the Your Photos section, and you'll now see your new set displayed on the right-hand side. Click on your new set, and you'll be taken to a page displaying the images residing within it. You can make various edits on this page, and by selecting View As Slideshow, you can display the images in Flash (you can copy and paste this link and send it to friends).

206 Organize your contacts

Under the Contacts link, you can add people in a number of ways. By selecting People Search, you can check whether friends are already using Flickr (by providing a name or email address). Alternatively, by selecting Invite Your Friends you can add three email addresses in the basic mode; or you can select Advanced, and enter a list of up to 100 comma-separated email addresses.

204 Share your set

If you like the idea of sharing a set, then there's a Share This Set link, that provides you with the option to send one of your sets to up to 50 different email addresses. Each address needs to be comma separated, and you can modify the message that recipients will see when they receive the mail.

207 Mappy talk

An interesting feature in the Organize section of Flickr is the Map. This enables you to geographically manage your photos (known as geotagging), and organize them according to where they were taken. To do this, you can highlight an area of the map and zoom in; alternatively, you can type a place name into the Find A Location box. Once you've found where an image was taken, drag the image onto the correct area.

205 Add To Faves

As you browse Flickr, you'll come across images that you want to keep. To the top left of every image you'll see an Add To Faves button, which will add any image to your favorites. These can then be accessed by selecting the You drop-down menu, and scrolling down to Your Favorites.

Flickr: take things further

208 Flickr Badge

The easiest way to add pictures to your blog or site is by using the Flickr Badge. While signed into Flickr, go to http://www.flickr.com/badge.gne. You'll be asked whether you want to go for a HTML or Flash Badge, so make your choice (we're going to opt for HTML).

209 Choose your photos

On the next page you'll be asked to choose the photos that you want to display. You can either display all your public photos, have them selected via tag, or choose a specific set. You can always change these settings later, so why not select the set you created earlier.

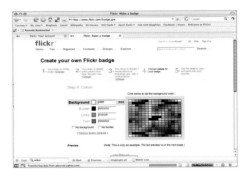

210 Badge layout

Next up is the Layout section. Here you can choose whether to add your Buddy Icon, choose how many photos you'd like to display, and specify a size; you can also select orientation. Select Next, and you'll now be taken to the area where you can change the colors of your Badge, and have them match your site or blog.

211 Get code

On the final page you'll be able to preview your new Badge, and a block of code will be displayed. You will need to copy this code and place it within your site or blog where you want your Badge to appear. This Badge will suit most people, but it doesn't offer much room for editing the appearance of your photos, so we're going to show you another way to display your pics.

212 Make your own

In the next few steps we'll show you how to have your Flickr photos display on your blog or site, but with more control than with the Flickr Badge. First, you'll need to create a Flickr web address. Select Your Account from the You menu, scroll down to Your Flickr Web Addresses and select Create Your Own Address. Now choose a URL, and select OK, Lock It In.

213 idGettr

To fetch Flickr images, you need to identify your Flickr ID (a number unique to your account). This can be a bit tricky within Flickr, but thankfully there's a website called idGettr, which fetches your ID for you. Head to http://idgettr.com, insert your new Flickr web address, and hit Find. Make a note of the returned ID.

214 Flickr tutorial

Developer Veerle Pieters (http://veerle.duoh.com) provides an excellent Flickr tutorial on her site, and we've taken her code and simplified it further for the purpose of this tutorial. The first thing you need to do is place the following code in your site (ensuring that you replace FLICKRURL with the URL you created in tip 212, and FLICKRID with the ID you got in tip 213).

```
<div id="flickr">
<p>Check out my <a href="http://www.flickr.com/photos/
YOURFLICKRURL/" target="_blank"><strong style="color:#3993ff">
flick<span style="color:#ff1c92">r</span></strong></a> photos</p>
<script type="text/javascript" src="http://www.flickr.com/badge_
code_
v2.gne?count=4&amp;display=random&amp;size=s&amp;layout=x&a
mp;source=user&amp;user=YOURFLICKRID"></script>
</div>
```

215 Style me up

That's the major work done. Now, we need to style our Flickr images. To do this you'll need to place three new CSS styles into your style sheet (in Blogger, you go to Edit HTML, and add it in the Edit Template section, with the rest of the CSS styles. (NOTE: This is the Flickr Div container.)

```
#flickr {
width:190px;
height:220px;
}
```

(NOTE: This controls your images, you can change width and height settings, but be sure to change the width and height settings in the Div container, too.)

```
#flickr img {
float:left;
border: none;
margin:0px 0px 5px 5px;
background:#000;
padding:1px;
width:85px;
height:85px;
}
```

(NOTE: This controls the text that appears over your photos. You can set your own font and size, and change the text as you wish.)

```
#flickr p {
font: 13px/1.5 "Lucida Grande," Lucida, Verdana,
sans-serif;
color: #000;
padding:0px 0px 0px 5px;
margin:5px 0px 5px 0px;
```

Cool tools

216 Flickr Uploadr

Uploading your photos manually via the Flickr site can be a bit time-consuming, but there are other options. First up, we'll look at Flickr Uploadr, which is available for both Mac OSX and Windows at http://www.flickr.com/tools/.

218 Uploadr settings

By default, Uploadr will scale the longest side of your image to 800 pixels; however, you can change these settings by going to Preferences in the Flickr Uploadr menu. Here you can change the upload dimensions, set the application to ask if it should resize an image over a certain size, or–if you want to munch through your 100MB monthly upload limit–you can set the software not to resize images at all. When you're done, select Upload.

217 Uploadr unleashed

Once you've downloaded and installed Flickr Uploadr, open the application. Now drag some photos into the section on the left, and a series of thumbnails will be generated. Select a thumbnail, and you'll be able to edit the individual properties of each image (you can also edit batch settings).

219 Flickr Finder

Unfortunately for PC users, this application is only for those running Mac OSX. And why is it unfortunate? Well, Flickr Finder enables you to search your Flickr images without accessing the site. First, visit http://gragsie.com/FlickrFinder/ and download the application. When you first open Flickr Finder you will have to authenticate the application.

220 Using Flickr Finder

Once you've authenticated Flickr Finder, the application will open. Your images will display in the right of the app, and as you select an image it will appear in the next pane (drag this pane to the right to increase the size of the photo). By default, details aren't displayed. To change this, go to Preferences, select the Photo Detail tab, and check all the options.

221 Flickr Sidebar

Considering our earlier praise for Firefox, it's only fitting we highlight a few of the great Flickr add-ons available to you. First up is the Flickr Sidebar. Flickr Sidebar enables you to view and search photo lists. You can open the menu at any time by pressing Ctrl+Shift+F on a PC, or Command+Shift+F on the Mac (you'll have to uninstall the Web Developer add-on though, for the hotkeys to work). Head over to https://addons.mozilla.org to get this add-on.

222 FlickrFox

If Flickr Sidebar doesn't meet your requirements, then why not try FlickrFox? FlickrFox does much the same thing as the Flickr Sidebar. Press Ctrl+7, and the sidebar will open (you'll then have to authenticate). Like Flickr Sidebar there's a search window, but you get more display options with this add-on.

223 PicLens

PicLens is a great way to view your Flickr photos in the appropriate manner, and that's full screen. Visit www.piclens.com/firefox and you can get your hands on the Firefox extension (only available for Firefox on the PC) or visit www.piclens.com/safari to get a Safari version for the Mac. Once installed, a little arrow will appear in the corner of all thumbnail images. Click it, and go full screen!

224 Flickr Slideshow Generator

Flickr provides you with the ability to embed Flash slideshows in your site, but it can be a bit tricky. Thankfully, Flickr Slideshow Generator enables you to create slideshows for all your photos, individual sets, groups, or tags. Select the question mark next to each input box, and there's information on how to find the right IDs. Visit www.fabiocavassini.com.ar/SlideShowGenerator.html to create yours.

225 Nostalgia

We've had a Mac-only application, so it's only fair that we repay the compliment for PC users. Nostalgia has been developed to show off Microsoft's new Windows Presentation Foundation (WPF) format. Put simply, it looks fantastic and enables you to manage many areas of your Flickr account from the desktop. To download, visit www.thirteen23.com/work/nostalgia/.

THE HENLEY COLLEGE LIBRARY

226 Upload by email

It's not always easy to get access to the Flickr site to upload your pictures–if you're using a cellphone, for instance–so the option to upload photos via email is one that many people will appreciate. While signed in, scroll to the bottom of the page and select Tools. To the right you'll see the Upload By Email link, click it.

 Upload by email

Email your photos directly to your photostream using a special upload by email address. (You can add tags and set privacy as you email as well. Handy!)

227 Getting your address

You'll now be taken to the Upload By Email page, and to the right you'll see your unique Flickr address. Any photo mailed to this address will be added to your photostream. Text in the subject will become the photo's title, text in the body the description, and you can add tags by putting "tags:" in the subject or body, and then adding your tags (if you add them to the body, you will need to start them on a new line).

Here's an example of adding tags in action.

Subject:	Lucy, my new cat tags: cute "black cat"
Body:	Lucy does the funniest dance moves! Isn't she cute?

Or you could send them in the body:

Subject:	Lucy, my new cat
	Lucy does the funniest dance moves!
Body:	Isn't she cute?
	tags: cute "black cat"

228 Go mobile!

If you want to access Flickr via your cellphone, you can. Simply open the browser in your phone and type m.flickr.com. The site is obviously more basic, but you can search photos, read comments, and check out photos posted by your contacts.

flickr
MOBILE SITE | Sign in

1 Photos from everyone
2 Explore recent photos

Search for photos:

text	tags

Your Privacy | Terms of Use
A Yahoo! company

229 Pretty bubbles

It's all well and good being serious–serious people are taken seriously after all. But we all need a laugh sometimes, and thanks to Bubblr (www.pimpampum. net/bubblr/) you can create comic strips from your photos. Either add your username or tags to get at your photos. Then just drag them into the main screen, and add some bubbles.

230 Flickr Show Licenses

This script enables you to see whether images have copyright applied to them, but you'll need to have Greasemonkey installed to take advantage of it. It shows licenses on all pages, and separates Creative Commons images from those with traditional copyright applied (Creative Commons images will have no logo, and copyrighted images will have a little symbol in the corner). Download the script here: http://userscripts.org/scripts/show/4099.

Eliza Carthy
Uploaded on 5 August 2006

 By Robby Garbett
See more photos, or visit his profile.

📷 beautiful, performers, ilford3200, kiss2
...

WOMAD Quakers for Peace
Uploaded on 17 November 2006

 By lostartist
See more photos, or visit lostartist's profile.

📷 world, uk, music, festival ...

231 Flickr Pro

Now we're going to look at what you get in the Pro Flickr account. For many, the monthly upload limit of 100MB, and the fact that you can't access your high-resolution photos, isn't a problem. But if you become a heavy Flickr user, you will start to consider paying out the annual fee for a Pro account.

233 Collections

If you're using a free account, you won't know what a Collection is, because you can't create them. Upgrade to Flickr Pro, and you can create Collections, which enable you to group your sets. Create a new Collection in the Organize section of Flickr, and then drag relevant sets into it.

232 Did we mention sets?

One of the major drawbacks of a free Flickr account is the fact that you're limited to just three sets. "So what?" you might say. But once you start uploading a lot of pictures, this limitation will seriously start to get on your nerves. Upgrade, and you can create as many sets as you like.

234 All sizes

Another reason to upgrade to Flickr Pro is the ability to access the full-size images you've uploaded. Although you can upload high-resolution images to a free Flickr account, you can't access them until you upgrade. Once you've upgraded, an All Sizes button will appear over every image, which will enable you to access your images in a selection of sizes.

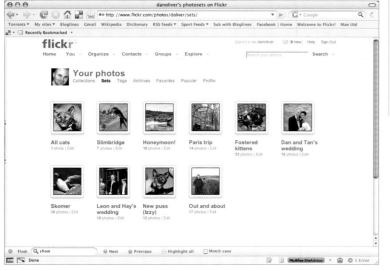

235 Everything unlimited

Although the benefits of a Flickr Pro account that we've already outlined are great, they're not the main reasons for upgrading. If you want one word that sums up the main reason for upgrading, it's this: unlimited. With a Flickr Pro account you get unlimited storage, unlimited uploads, and unlimited bandwidth.

Facebook

There's a networking site creating some serious waves on the net, and that site is Facebook. Initially, Facebook was launched as a social network for students at Harvard University (in the US, "facebook" is the term for a publication made of students' names and faces, intended to help students get to know each other better); however, in September 2006 the Facebook team opened membership up to any email address. The site, created by then-student Mark Zuckerberg, enables you to create a network of friends and family, and share all manner of information with them. Whether you want to share photos, review your favorite movies, upload video, or play a quick game of Scrabble, Facebook can oblige. And with its own API available to developers, there are hundreds of fantastic applications available via Facebook, the best of which we'll cover in this chapter. So, even if you already have an account, we guarantee that you'll find something new!

Facebook basics

236 Sign up to Facebook

The first thing you need to do is sign up at www.facebook.com. You'll need to provide your name, state whether you're working or in education, supply your date of birth, and answer a security ou'll now be sent a confirmation email.

237 Add friends

One of the keys to Facebook's success is the ease with which you can add friends, and inform those that aren't already on Facebook that you've signed up. Once you've confirmed your new account, you'll be taken to a page titled Find Your Friends On Facebook.

238 Provide your details

If you use one of the major, free email providers (such as Gmail, Yahoo!, AOL, or MSN) then all you need to do is enter your email address and password, and Facebook will then search the network to find which of your contacts are already on there. If you don't use one of these services, don't worry. We'll show you how to add an existing address book later.

239 Adding Friends

The next page will inform you how many of your contacts are already on Facebook. By default all of these names will be checked, but we recommend unchecking the Select All box at the top of the list, and then checking the box next to those people you'd like to add.

240 Invite to join

On the next page you'll see a list of your contacts that aren't currently on Facebook. At this point you should definitely uncheck the Select All/None box at the top of the page. The last thing people need is more junk in their inboxes, and many of the people in your contacts won't have a clue who you are. Find close friends and family–who won't mind being hassled–and check the box next to their name. Then select Invite To Join.

241 Add from address book

Not everyone uses an online email account, so Facebook enables you to upload an existing address book to check for friends. Select the drop-down arrow next to the Friends link at the top of the page, and scroll to Find Friends. On this page you'll see a link called Email Application; click it. A window will now open, enabling you to navigate to your address book on your hard drive.

242 I have no contact file!

Don't worry if you have no contact file saved, as Facebook has all the answers. Select the Read How To Create A Contact File link, and a drop-down will show you how to create one for all the major desktop email packages. Once you've followed these instructions, locate the file, and Facebook will check for signed up friends.

243 Other search options

Hopefully, some of your friends are already on Facebook, and you've now started to build a Friends list. However, one of the great things about Facebook is catching up with old friends, whose email addresses you may no longer have. To search for old buddies simply enter their name in the Search window to the top left of the screen.

244 Narrow your search

With the amount of people on Facebook, you may need to narrow down your search. First, go to the Friends drop-down, scroll to Find Friends, click the More Ways To Find Friends link at the bottom of the page, and select one of the links (school, university, coworker). Now you can add a few more details, which should narrow things down.

245 Friend detail requests

Because people need to approve your requests to add them to your Friends list, it'll take a little while before people start getting back to your initial invites. You'll be notified when friends get back to you, and these notifications will appear in the top right of your Facebook page. Select the Friend Detail Request link.

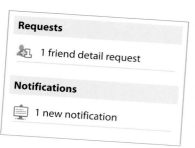

246 Approve or ignore

This isn't just where your invited friends will appear, it's also where people inviting you will show up. Either way, once a Friend Detail Request arrives, you must decide whether to Confirm or Reject (Accept or Ignore, if someone is trying to add you to their list).

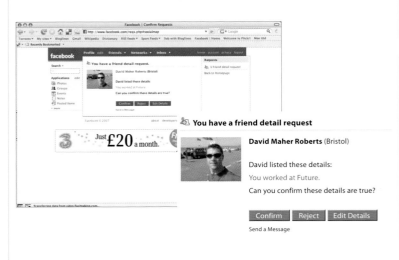

247 Edit details

Facebook is all about listing your "Friends," and also your relationship to them. You can leave details blank if you wish, but by selecting the Edit Details box, you can provide more information on how you know each other, which is useful for other applications in Facebook (which we'll look at later).

248 Profile picture

By default, the only information about you that Facebook shows to those people that search for you is your name and location, and with millions of people using Facebook, there could be plenty of people with your name out there! To help people searching, and to jazz up your Facebook account, you should add a Profile picture. To do this select the Edit link next to Profile.

249 A good pic

Before you upload an image, you should make sure that there's a pretty tight crop on your face (after all, you want people to be able to recognize you). We suggest creating an image at 200 pixels wide, as this is the largest size your image will display at (smaller thumbnails of the same image will appear elsewhere on the site). When you have a pic, select Picture from the menu in the Edit section, and browse to a picture you'd like to upload, finally selecting Upload Picture.

250 The thumbnail

Once you've uploaded your image, you can then drag your photo within the Thumbnail Version window, so you get the crop you want on the smaller profile picture, which will appear on the site. Once you're happy with the positioning, select Save Thumbnail Version.

Thumbnail Version

Drag the image to adjust:
We use this version of your picture around the site.

Save Thumbnail Version

251 Further Profile edits

While we're in the Edit section of the Profile, let's look at some other areas. First, select Basic from the submenu. Here you can enter all manner of information (whether you're married, what your political views are, etc.), but the main area–especially for people worried about identity theft–is the option to not display your birthday. Under Birthday, select the drop-down, and choose from Show, Show Month & Day, Don't Show.

252 Contact and Personal

The Contact details you provide are up to you, and we'll explain about security later in this chapter (at which point you can always change the details you provide). As for the Personal section, here you can provide all manner of information on yourself, including your favorite movies, music that you love, quotes that inspire you, and much more.

253 Education and Work

In these two sections, you have the option to provide more information about your background. This enables former coworkers and schoolmates to catch up with you, much as they would by using a site such as Friends Reunited.

254 Facebook Layout

Don't worry! We're not going to get back into the kind of editing that was required within Blogger, but this doesn't mean you can't modify the look and feel of your Facebook site a little. If you select the main Profile link, you can simply drag and drop elements where you would like them to appear. There are some restrictions, and users of MySpace may feel fettered, but with so many add-ons and page elements within Facebook, providing a carte blanche with the design could lead to some horrific looking pages.

255 The Friends page

We're going to assume that a little time has passed, and you now have a Facebook account populated with Friends. If you select the Friends link at the top of your Facebook page, by default you'll be shown a list of your Friends who have recently updated their pages.

256 More Friends options

If you select the Show drop-down menu in the Friends section, you can display all your friends, those currently online, and select from a host of other choices. You can also go through the process of checking your address book again by choosing Find Friends from the menu. Lastly, you can even access a Social Timeline, which takes the information you added about your friends, and creates a year-by-year view of your relationships.

257 Messaging friends

There are Send Message links all over Facebook, and a good way to send messages is to find your Friend by selecting All Friends from the Show drop-down menu, and then selecting the Send Message link to the right of your friend's details. Having selected this link a new message window will open. Your new message will appear in your friend's inbox when they next log in.

258 Notifications

Whenever someone sends you a message, or interacts with your Facebook account in almost any way, you'll be sent a Notification. By default these will also be sent to your primary email address, but you can always access them by selecting the drop-down menu next to the Inbox link, and scrolling down to Notifications.

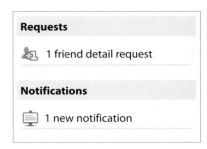

259 Your Inbox

Messaging is an integral part of Facebook, and all messages are stored in your Inbox (including Notifications, as we've just discussed). By selecting the main Inbox link you'll be taken directly to your messages. In this section you can also access Sent Messages, and if you look to the right you'll see the Compose Message link.

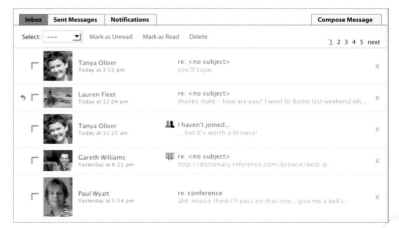

260 The bits down the side

Now we've covered the main sections within Facebook, let's take a quick look at some of the default applications (we'll cover applications in more detail later in the chapter). These applications reside on the far left of your screen, and are only ever one click away, no matter which section you're in.

Applications edit

Photos

Groups

Events

Notes

Posted Items

▼ more

262 Add photos

Once you've created an album, you'll be taken to the next section, where you can manage your photos. There's a pretty familiar tree structure that enables you to browse your hard drive for images, and it's probably best to organize the pictures you want to upload into one folder. When you've found your images, make sure they are selected, and rotate them if need be. Finally, select Upload.

261 Create an album

One of the most popular aspects of Facebook is the ability to add photo albums to your page. When you select the Photos link the first screen will show you a list of recent photo albums added by friends (you can also see where your friends have been tagged in other photos). To create your own album, select the Add New Photos button (to the top right), provide album details (choosing whether to make them available to everyone or just friends), and select Create Album.

263 It's not Flickr

Be warned, Facebook's photo support is fairly limited, and this isn't a service for archiving your photos. No matter what the size, your photos will be resized on the fly as you upload them, and the resulting images will be poorer quality (fine for sharing with friends, but not good enough for an archive). Once photos are uploaded you can provide captions, and also choose which image you'd like to use as an album cover. When you're done, hit Save Changes.

264 Tagging

At any point you can edit and manage your new album, but one of the things you'll be taking most advantage of is tagging. When you select an image, a menu appears beneath it (this isn't just for photos in your album, it's for all photos). Select Tag This Photo and a crosshair will appear, enabling you to draw a square over part of the image. When you do this a list of all your contacts will display, and if the name doesn't appear then just type it in the window. When you're finished, hit Done Tagging.

Facebook security

So far we've highlighted some of the basic functions in Facebook, but before we go any further we need to offer up a few security tips. Millions of people are now using Facebook, and any platform as popular as this will have unsavory people—we'll call them criminals—trying to take advantage of it. We'll now reveal how to tighten your security on Facebook (many of these recommendations are courtesy of security company Sophos at www.sophos.com).

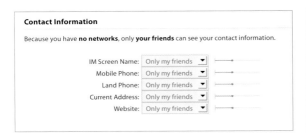

265 Profile settings

By default, it's not just your friends that can see your profile, anyone else in the same network can also see it. As you have no control over who's in the networks you join, you should select the Privacy link to the top right, head into the Profile settings, and select Only My Friends from the first drop-down.

266 Other Profile settings

While still in the Profile section of the Privacy settings, you'll see a group of settings that include: Videos Tagged Of You, Photos Tagged Of You, Online Status, and Wall. Your Online Status should be set to Only My Friends as a minimum setting, but there's no reason you can't choose No One (is it really that important that others know when you're on Facebook?). The rest of these options can be set to Only My Friends.

267 Contact info and apps

We're still editing the privacy settings within the Profile, and first up is Contact Information. Despite Facebook enabling the option for friends and people in your network to see your contact info, we suggest you set all of these to No One (barring the website, which you can display to friends). After all, any of your friends in Facebook can easily message you, so why make all this information available? As for Applications, set the viewing rights to Only My Friends.

268 Search settings

Now, while in the Privacy section, select Search from the menu. Facebook is all about finding people, so you can select Everyone under Who Can Find Me In Search; however, ensure you don't check the box below, allowing anyone to see your public search listing.

269 What can searchers do?

At the bottom of the Search settings screen you'll see a list of things that people can do once they've found you in a search. When you respond to messages and pokes then your profile can be viewed by the sender for a limited period. To ensure you don't give any information away, uncheck the boxes next to Send You A Message, Poke You, and View Your Friend List. Check the boxes next to See Your Picture and Add You As A Friend, so people can still search for you, and put a face to your name.

270 News Feed and Mini Feed

Select the News Feed and Mini Feed link in the Privacy section. By default, a lot of things you do on Facebook are passed on to your friends via their News Feeds. In this section you can select the actions within Facebook that result in an update being published to the feeds of you and your friends. No one wants to hear everything you're doing, so choose wisely.

271 Poke, Message, and Friend Request

When you contact someone via a poke, message, or friend request, you can set what information they'll see. So, if an identity thief messages you, and you reply asking who they are, you could be inadvertently opening yourself up. To avoid such a scenario, go into the Poke, Message, and Friend Request settings, and make sure only Basic Info is selected.

272 Applications

Many of the applications on Facebook are developed by third-party developers, so you should be mindful of the information you're providing. If you select Applications from the Privacy section, you'll see that you can edit the settings for Notes and Photos. Select the Privacy Settings link next to either, and set them to be viewed by Only My Friends.

273 Block People

Chances are that your Facebook experience will be a happy one, but if someone starts bothering you, you can simply add them to an Ignore list. At the bottom of the main Privacy section you'll see a box titled Block People. Just write the name of the person you want to ignore in this box.

Facebook applications

What sets Facebook apart from other social networks is the support it offers for third parties who wish to create applications for the Facebook platform. By making its API available to developers, Facebook has ensured that the platform won't stagnate, and will hopefully retain its users. In the next pages we're going to look at the best of the bunch, because there's a lot of garbage out there, too!

274 Flickr Photosets

Select the Applications link in the menu to the left, now choose Browse More Applications. Now type Flickr in the search window, and choose Flickr Photosets. Having added the application, you'll be asked to specify what you want the app to do (such as whether you want it to publish new updates in your News Feed).

275 Authenticate and add photos

Having chosen your preferences, you'll have to authenticate the application at Flickr. Hit the Authenticate button, and you'll be taken to the Flickr login page. Once you've logged in, select the OK I'll Allow It button (you'll now be taken back to Facebook). On the next screen select your privacy settings (we suggest you only display photos to Facebook friends), and you can also specify what images will display (via tags or date). Now, go into your profile, and your Flickr photos will be on display.

276 Scrabulous

As Jack Nicholson famously wrote, "All work and no play makes Jack a dull boy." In keeping with Jack's sentiments, we'd like to introduce Scrabulous. As one of Facebook's biggest hits to date, this application enables you to play Scrabble online. Just type Scrabulous in the application search window, and follow the instructions. It's worth noting that there are two main dictionaries: one for North America—TWL—and one for everyone else—Sowpods.

277 Cities I've Visited

Remember when booking accommodation abroad was a total lottery? Thankfully, companies such as TripAdvisor (www.tripadvisor.com) enable us to share our experiences. Cities I've Visited is a Facebook application from TripAdvisor, which enables you to tell your friends where you've been. Just search for Cities I've Visited in the application search window.

278 Video

Although you can embed YouTube videos in Facebook, there's also the option of uploading your video straight to the site. And if you want to view any of these videos, then you'll also need to install the application. To add the video app just type Video into the application search, and select Add Video. To add or record video select the Video link, under your Applications on the right of the screen, and select the Upload/Record tab.

279 Books iRead

This handy app enables you to show others what you're reading, list what's in your collection, and highlight the tomes you'd like to get your hands on. Having installed iRead, select it from your applications list. Now just search for a book, and when the results are returned you can select Reading It, Read It, or Wanna Read It.

280 Flixter

Everyone likes to think they'd make a good movie reviewer, and thanks to Flixter you can put your journalistic skills to the test (and show off your movie know-how to your friends). This isn't just a vanity app, though, as it enables you to gauge the movies your friends are enjoying, and hopefully help you avoid the turkeys. Search for a movie, rate it, and review it: simple!

281 Top Friends

Using the Top Friends application, you can select 32 of your closest friends, and have their profile pictures appear in a bar at the side of the page, thus ensuring that they're only ever one click away. Once you've added the application, the next screen enables you to set options. It's probably best that you don't display the Top Friends app in your Profile or News Feed, as there will likely be people you omit who could take offence.

282 Facebook Toolbar

Thanks to the development team at Facebook, you can now add a number of Facebook tools to your web browser—so long as you're using Firefox. Visit http://developers.facebook.com/toolbar/, and select Download Facebook Toolbar. When you restart your browser, you'll see a new toolbar, with a number of new icons (see the image below). Now, you no longer need to be on Facebook to stay up-to-date with your friends.

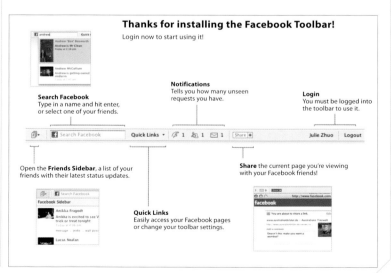

285 Drag to reorder

If you want to edit your installed applications at any point, simply select the Applications link on the left. In the main window you'll see all your apps—with Edit Settings links next to them—but if you look to the left you'll also notice that you can reorder your applications. Just drag and drop them to your liking, but be aware that you can only ever have seven apps that are always on show.

283 Friends sidebar

One of the best features of the Facebook Toolbar is the Facebook Friends Sidebar. By selecting the icon on the far left of the toolbar, you will open up a new window, which lists all of the people in your Friends list. You can then send a message, poke, or write a wall post, directly from this window.

286 Bobbleheads

This is possibly the most immature application we'll cover—though there are plenty to choose from—but we couldn't pass up the opportunity of adding a nodding Dog the Bounty Hunter to our Profile. Once you've installed Bobbleheads, you can choose from a host of celebrities, who will offer words of wisdom as you click their heads.

284 iLike

If you're a music fan, then you may already be aware of the iLike add-on for iTunes. The iLike Facebook application isn't quite as good as the iTunes original, but it does enable you to see who's into the same music as you, who's playing in concert, and who's producing free music in the same style as your preferred artists.

287 Fish, zombies, and other assorted nonsense

Facebook has lots of useful apps, but it has just as many pointless ones. Though fun when you first start using the platform, the thirtieth request you get to join someone's zombie army may start to get on your nerves. We're not saying don't use them, just be mindful of how many invites you're sending out.

288 My Questions

The My Questions application enables you to ask a question of all your friends on Facebook. You can gauge opinion on any topic of your choosing, and have it display on your profile and Feeds. To add a new question simply select the My Questions link under your apps, and write one.

slide My Questions

Ask more Questions with FunWall! | Help

Ask a Question | My Questions | Friends' Questions | Cool Apps

Ask your own question:

Is a Kit Kat a chocolate-covered biscuit, or a biscuit-centered chocolate bar?

This question will be posted on your profile.
(178 characters remaining)

Our suggestions:

○ Which part of your body do you love to show off the most?
○ What one thing did you learn today?
○ What's the most embarrassing thing that's happened to you on a date?

○ I don't want to ask a question today

OK

289 PacMan

We may have highlighted the dangers of using too many fun apps, but PacMan isn't just about fun, it's much more serious than that– it's a piece of geek history! Install the PacMan application, and you can play the classic game from within Facebook by selecting it from your menu (control PacMan with the arrow keys).

290 Recipe Binder

We love this application, but then we love food! Once you've installed Recipe Binder–and this is one of the few apps that didn't bug us about inviting friends–you'll be greeted with a screen featuring five tabs (Find Recipes, Most Recent, Top Rated, My Recipes, and Add A Recipe). You can either find recipes, add them to be viewed by other Facebook users, or just add them to your private recipe section. Yummy!

291 Sticky Notes

There are plenty of ways to leave messages for friends, but one of the most obvious ways is to use the Sticky Notes application. Once you've installed it, you'll be able to choose the color of your Notes, the font you want to use, the font color, and then type your message. Select the Preview button, and you'll see your new Note and a window where you can add a friend's details (if they don't have the app installed, they'll be invited).

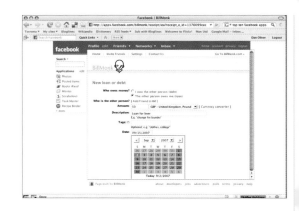

294 BillMonk

If you never lend anyone money, then you can skip this step. But for the more generous among you, the BillMonk application enables you to keep tabs on the cash you are due, and that which you owe. If you don't already have a BillMonk account, you'll have to sign up for one before you can get started.

292 My Personality

According to the guys behind My Personality, this application enables you to answer questions "from a real psychological personality questionnaire, see the explanation of your results, and then compare yourself to your friends." You'll need to answer around 20 questions, then prepare for the truth–if you can handle it! You can answer more questions if you want a more accurate result.

295 My Files

Box.net has developed My Files for Facebook, enabling Facebook users to store files online via the platform (including photos, video, and music), or even share files with other users (taking advantage of Box.net's free storage). You start off with 10MB of space by default, and get more as more of your friends sign up (existing users can get up to 1GB of storage).

293 Task Master

When it comes to GTD–or getting things done, for the uninitiated– the apps don't get much better than Task Master from Dave Langer and Stuart Starr. This application isn't complicated, and all it does is enable you to create to-do lists, but it does it brilliantly. Once installed, head to your Task Master page, and you'll see an Add New Task button, select this to add a new item. On the next page you can offer a description, add a due date, and invite other Facebook users to the task.

296 Zoho Online Office

Zoho offers a host of office tools online, and this application enables you to build them into Facebook. Once installed, you can access your existing Zoho projects, or create new ones from within Facebook.

297 del.icio.us

We've already shown you how you can improve your online experience by employing social bookmarking via del.icio.us, and it won't come as a surprise that there's a Facebook application that enables you to get at your del.icio.us links. You'll have to add your del.icio.us account details, and allow Facebook to access your links (links can be displayed as most recent, or as a tag cloud).

298 myRSS

Rather than use an external feed reader, you can view all your feeds from within Facebook (though it's nothing like as powerful as Bloglines). Unfortunately, you'll have to add feeds individually, but it's another neat application for those who can't bear the thought of leaving Facebook's walled garden.

299 Graffiti

With the Graffiti application, you can add a small section to your profile, which your friends can access, and then vandalize to their hearts' content. This is all well and good if you have trustworthy friends; however, if your buddies are the kind of people that still put plastic wrap over the toilet seat, it may be best to pass on this app!

300 Tetris Tournament

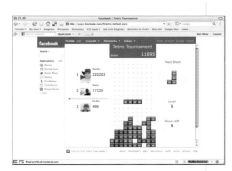

Like Pacman, Tetris is a piece of gaming history. If, like us, you've actually dreamt about Tetris at some point in the past, you'll spend far too long on this game than you should. For the more normal among you, it's a great distraction. You can play on your own or against your friends.

301 Training

Facebook can give you the body of a Greek Adonis. Well, that's not entirely true. But what it can do is enable you to list your chosen exercise regime, so that you can swap tips–and exchange some much needed encouragement–with friends.

Facebook hacks: take things further

302 Greasemonkey and Firefox

With Greasemonkey installed on Firefox, there are some very cool Facebook hacks you can employ, including things such as the ability to automatically login, inbox notification, and more! If you don't have the Greasemonkey add-on installed within Firefox then head over to https://addons.mozilla.org.

303 Facebook Video

Facebook provides the option to share and upload video, but you're essentially locked into the Facebook app. The Facebook Video script for Greasemonkey enables you to download video, convert it, and embed files into other sites. Go to http://userscripts.org/scripts/show/9789, select Install Script on the right, and restart Firefox. Now when you go back into Facebook, you'll see new options under any videos.

```
Share +

Report Video
Download Video
Convert Video

Embed Code
<embed type="application/x-sh
```

304 Quick Links

Want to add a new menu item to the top of the Facebook interface? With Quick Links you can add a new drop-down menu next to Inbox, which enables you to access pages within Facebook quickly. Go to http://userscripts.org/scripts/show/11208, and install the script. Open Facebook, and you'll see a new Add A Link item above your profile on the right. You'll be asked to give the link a name and provide a URL. A new link now appears to the right.

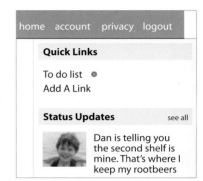

305 Where's the drop-down?

Something we should point out is that the drop-down menu will only appear when you navigate away from your main Feed page (where Quick Links appear on the right). Away from the Feed page you'll see a new menu item at the top of Facebook titled qLink: add new links by selecting it, scrolling down to the bottom of the list, and selecting qLink This Page.

306 Facebook Message Alert

Worried about missing messages in Facebook? Thankfully, ms609 (that's a username) over at Userscripts.org has created a script that makes your Inbox pulse orange when you have a message. This won't suit everyone, but you won't be able to miss new messages.

309 inYOFYceBook

You may not always want to click through to view images on Facebook, and this useful script enables you to rollover thumbnails and profile pictures to view larger versions of the images. To get your hands on this script, already being used by thousands of other Facebook hackers, go to http://userscripts.org/scripts/show/8712.

310 Facebook Color Changer

Facebook and MySpace couldn't be more different when it comes to their approach to design: MySpace enables you to create the most hideous sites on the planet, while Facebook exerts a vice-like grip over its design. Thanks to the script at http://userscripts.org/scripts/show/9475, though, you can now do a little modifying of Facebook with the ability to change background colors and the site logo. To make edits, go to Tools>Greasemonkey>User Script Commands> Customize Facebook Colors.

307 Facebook Companion

Not only does this script remove adverts from your Facebook account, it also provides a small plus symbol on all images in Facebook, which you can select to see the full-size image. It's not the most natural combination, but it does both things well. You can find the script at http://userscripts.org/scripts/show/8475.

308 Facebook Auto-Login

Despite Firefox having the option to remember your Facebook login details, Facebook still occasionally asks that you provide sign-in details (which can be a pain). However, head on over to http://userscripts.org/scripts/show/10560, and you can install a script that will log you straight in (saving you valuable seconds in Scrabulous).

311 Facebook Auto-Colorizer

The last hack we're going to look at is one that many people will avoid like the plague. We've already mentioned MySpace, and how you can edit far more using it as a platform, and this next script brings much more color to Facebook. Install the script at http://userscripts.org/scripts/show/3626, and your pages, including Friend profiles, will be colored depending on the photo on the page. Check it out!

YouTube

YouTube has revolutionized video on the internet by making it easy to put your videos online, share clips, and search for uploads from other users. By encoding videos in Flash, the majority of net users can view YouTube content, with no need to download an extra plug-in. According to Adobe—the company responsible for Flash—more than 800 million people now have a version of the Flash Player installed. It's this concentration on ease-of-use that has helped YouTube to progress, and when Google acquired the company for $1.65 billion at the end of 2006, YouTube's founders Steve Chen, Chad Hurley, and Jawed Karim became very rich men. In this chapter, we'll show you what all the fuss is about.

YouTube basics

312 Set up an account

Let's start by visiting www.youtube.com and setting up an account (although you can view content without one, to unleash the full potential of YouTube you should create one). First, select Sign Up from the top right.

313 Types of account

There are five accounts to choose from. A regular account enables you to upload, share, search, and comment; a director account lets you do things such as add a logo to your profile page; a musician or comedian account enables customization, and the option to provide CD purchase links, and the like; and last—but by no means least—the guru account makes it possible to add custom logos, genres, and links on your profile page. For now, choose a Standard account, and fill in the rest of the details.

314 Getting to know YouTube

Before we look at the exciting opportunities YouTube offers for those of you wanting to upload your own video, let's take a look at what's already available. At the top of the site is a text field where you type your search terms. When results are returned, you can view them by Date Added, View Count, and Rating.

315 Viewing a video

After selecting the link for the video you want to watch, you'll be taken to a new page. The first thing to point out are the standard video controls–play/pause, rewind, volume, and full screen mode–but that's just the start. Below the video you can give it a rating, and see the comments posted by others.

316 Favorites

Next to the star ratings, you'll see a selection of links. The first link is Save To Favorites, which enables you to bookmark the videos you think you'd like to view at a later date. Once you've selected the link, a window opens where you can choose to save a video to a playlist. As you have no playlists, select the drop-down, select New Playlist, and hit OK.

317 Add to video log

Having created the new playlist, the next screen enables you to give the playlist a name, set whether it's public or private, provide a description and tags, and specify whether this playlist will be your Video Log. A Video Log is essentially a blog of movie clips, and by selecting this option you enable all the videos placed in this playlist to de displayed in your Profile.

318 Accessing playlists

Once you've added some videos to a playlist, you can then access them via a selection of links to the right on the front page (if you're not on the front page then select My Account, and use the links to the top right).

319 Profile page

If you look to the top of the YouTube interface, you'll see your username as a link. Select this, and you'll be taken to your profile page. Here the videos you upload will be displayed, your Playlists can be viewed, and others can get in touch with you. For others to find you all they need to do is visit www.youtube.com/YOURUSERNAME.

320 General Messages

By selecting the little envelope next to your username, at the top of the interface, you can access the General Messages section. Here you'll be able to exchange messages with other YouTube users, and also receive things such as invites to YouTube groups.

321 My Account

Select the My Account link at the top of the page, and you'll be taken to the main place for you to manage all your YouTube activity. There's a lot to take in via this section, and we'll revisit some of the main areas later in the chapter. For now, it's about time we uploaded a video.

322 Video support

Before you upload any videos there are a few things you need to remember. The first is that YouTube has support for certain file types, while eschewing others. However, this isn't to say that your videos won't upload, because the formats that YouTube supports are those supported by most digital video recorders. The supported formats are WMV, AVI, MOV, and MPG.

323 Optimize your video

One of the main gripes people have with YouTube is the quality of the video on the site. Much of this is down to YouTube's encoding—which YouTube claims is to make videos available to as many people as possible—but there are ways to improve the quality. YouTube claims that video should be saved as MPEG4 (Divx, Xvid), should be 320 x 240 resolution, should include MP3 audio, and should run at 30 frames per second. You can use software such as Final Cut Pro or Toast Titanium to change video settings.

324 Some size information

All the videos uploaded to YouTube must be 100MB or less. The longer your video, the more compression is required to make it fit into the same file size. Because of this, the best quality videos are usually around five minutes or less, with a maximum limit of 10 minutes for videos.

325 Upload

When your movie is ready to upload, select the Upload link, which is always visible to the top right of the YouTube site. On the next page you will have to provide your video with a title, description, tags, and specify a category that's most suited to your clip.

326 Select video

On the next screen you'll need to browse to the video you want to upload on your hard drive. Once you've found it, select the clip, and then hit the Upload Video button. A message will then display, and you'll have to wait until it has left the screen before you can navigate away from the page.

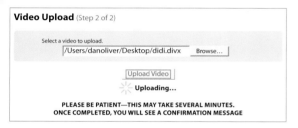

327 Copyright

While you're waiting for your video to upload, it's worth pointing out that all the videos you upload to YouTube are subject to its terms. To make things safe, you shouldn't upload any video that you don't own the copyright for (if you have express permission from the owner of the copyright, you can also upload clips). You can find a full list of terms at http://www.youtube.com/t/terms.

Kitten tries on my size nines

328 Upload Complete

Once your video has been added you'll get an Upload Complete message. As well as a completion message, you'll also be supplied with code that you can copy and paste into a website, should you wish to embed the video somewhere other than YouTube. Also, you can now access the video by going into My Accounts and selecting My Videos.

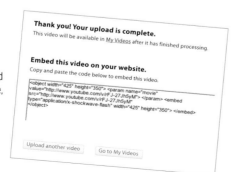

329 That's quality!

The video we took for our kitten-inspired clip wasn't taken on a particularly good video camera (in fact, it was taken using the video function on a Canon digital camera). However, using the settings that we've outlined here, you'll notice that the video quality is better than most of those clips that you'll see on YouTube. You can go here to watch the video: http://www.youtube.com/ahdanielsan

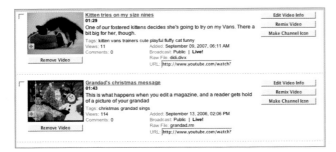

330 My Videos

Select the Go To My Videos button at the bottom of the completion page, and you'll be able to see your uploaded videos. In this page you'll get various information on your video, such as the details you provided (which can be edited by selecting the Edit Video Info button), a link so you can distribute your video, and the option to remix and remove your videos as well.

331 History

As you start to view more videos, it's easy to forget to add them to Playlists, or make them Favorites. Thankfully, YouTube has a History section that you can access via the link at the top of the site, where you can view the latest videos you've watched. And, if you're worried about privacy, you can always clear your history in this section, too.

332 Quicklist

While you're in the history section, you may also notice a link titled Quicklist. If you're in a hurry and don't have time to save videos in Playlists or as Favorites, you can simply click the little + symbol that appears on all videos on YouTube. Then, at your own leisure, you can get to them via the Quicklist (this will also display as a list under YouTube videos).

333 Active Sharing

Another section that falls under the History link is Active Sharing. If you're one of those people that likes others to be able to see what you've been viewing then you'll love Active Sharing, because that's exactly what it does.

334 Updates

By now, some people may have started watching your videos, and maybe even commenting on them. Because it's hard to keep tabs on everything you do online, by default YouTube will send you email alerts every time one of your videos gets a comment, so you never miss out on what people are saying.

335 Remixer

In My Videos you'll see a Remix button to the right of all your videos. By selecting this, you can try out one of YouTube's coolest new features (courtesy of Adobe). Once you've selected the Remix Video button you'll have to wait a few seconds for the page to load, after which your videos will display to the right. Drag one of them into the main area on the left.

337 Borders

If you want to add even more of a personal feel to your video then there's also the option to add a border. There are some slightly cheesier options, such as hearts for Valentine videos, but there are also some classy-looking borders, too (though we discounted those, and went for a billboard!). Once you're happy with your new video, select Publish (your original won't be deleted, so don't worry). At the time of writing there was no option to add music, but it was earmarked to be "coming soon."

338 Find out more

Once you've spent a bit of time on YouTube, you'll realize that certain people on the network are fanatical about specific subjects, and as such they search out the best videos in that area. To visit a YouTube user's Profile page, simply select their name next to any videos they've posted.

From: RedDevil111
Views: 78,007
Added: 1 year ago
More in Sports

336 Graphics and captions

Where many people will be happy simply uploading video, many of you will love these options. If you select Graphics and Captions from the menu on the right, you'll see a host of things—such as captions and thought bubbles—that can be dragged to your video, and edited to suit your requirements.

339 View and Subscribe

Once you're on a member's Profile page, you can view the videos in their shared Playlists, and also see the videos they've uploaded. Also, if you think you'd like to see what they upload in the future, you can select the orange Subscribe button, which will then add any new videos from that user to the My Subscriptions page under My Account.

YouTube: take things further

340 Add blog

If you have a blog, then YouTube has excellent features that enable you to post clips directly to your third-party blog. At the moment the supported platforms are Blogger, Wordpress, LiveJournal, Friendster, Piczo, and Freewebs. To get started, go into My Account, scroll down to your Account Settings, and select Video Posting Settings.

341 Choose your platform

You'll now see a selection of the supported blogging platforms. If you don't already have a blog, then select one of the logos; however, if you do have a blog, then click the Add A Blog/Site button. Now choose your blogging service from the drop-down, and enter your username and password. YouTube will now fetch your blog details.

342 Add your blog

Once your blog details have been retrieved you'll be taken to a screen that features your blog's name, URL, and also has an empty checkbox to the left. Select this box, and then select Add Selected Blogs. Your blog will now be added to YouTube, and you can edit the details by returning to Video Posting settings at any time.

343 Add video to your blog

Now, adding video to your blog couldn't be simpler. Beneath any video that you watch you'll see a selection of links (where you can rate the video), and among them is the Post Video link. Select Post Video, choose your blog from the drop-down, add title and description information, and hit Post To Blog. The video will now appear on your site.

344 The custom player

YouTube enables you to display a selection of videos in a customized player (your videos, a playlist, or your favorites), which can then be embedded elsewhere (or sent to others). The first thing you need to do is go into My Account, scroll down to Custom Players, and select Create Custom Player.

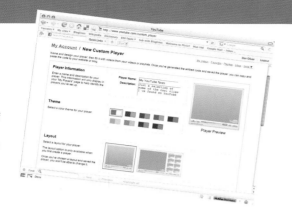

345 Get creative

On the next screen you are able to modify the name, description, and appearance of your player, as well as specifying a preferred layout. Rather than give you all the colors of the web to choose from, the YouTube team has provided some classic color combinations, and when it comes to layout you can opt for the classic view, or have a list of videos displayed to the side of the player.

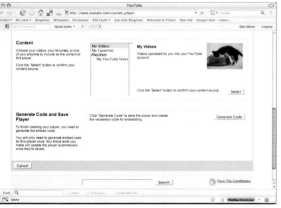

346 Generate code

Having specified the look of your player, you now need to select which videos you want to display; you can choose from My Videos, My Favorites, or one of your existing playlists. The last thing you need to do is select the Generate Code button, which will provide you with the code that you need to add to your site or blog.

347 Go mobile

With an increasing number of cellphones now supporting video they have become one of the main ways that people capture movies. With this in mind, YouTube has its very own mobile service, where you can upload clips directly from your phone. To get started, go into My Account, scroll to Account Settings, and select Mobile Profile.

348 Create Mobile Profile

Before you can post videos from your phone you'll have to create a Mobile Profile, so select the Create Mobile Profile button. Now you'll need to provide some details. YouTube requires your cellphone number (with country code), your provider details, a title that will be added to all videos from your phone, and tags that you want assigned to your clips. When you've entered these details you will be provided with a unique MMS email identity, where you will then need to send your clips.

349 Get tooled up

Hopefully, you've now got a good understanding of what YouTube has to offer, but this doesn't mean your YouTube experience can't be improved further. There are a host of third parties developing great applications and tools for YouTube, and here we'll look at the best. To see a selection of the third party developments YouTube recommends visit http://www.youtube.com/dev.

350 Download YouTube clips

If you'd like to download a YouTube video clip to your hard drive–to view it on a portable media player, for example–there are a number of online services that do the job. However, the best we've found is Vixy.net. Simply copy and paste the URL of the YouTube video you'd like to download, and place it in the URL window at www.vixy.net. Now, select the video you want to convert to from the drop-down, and select Start.

351 Convert and download

Vixy.net will now convert the FLV movie–the Flash file which YouTube uses–into your preferred movie format. Once Vixy.net has made the conversion, you will be provided with a link where you can now download the converted movie from.

352 YouTube badge

The badge creator at http://flashandburn.net/youtubeBadge/ will generate a PNG graphic of the last six videos that you uploaded to YouTube. This isn't much use if you're not making many YouTube clips, but if you're a regular poster then it's a great way to keep people updated with your newest additions. Add your username at the site, select Get Code, and then paste the returned code into your site (you'll also get a preview).

353 YouTube Maximize

This Greasemonkey script for Firefox adds a "maximize" link on top of YouTube videos, so you don't have to use the built-in maximize button. This means that you can get more control over the video that you're maximizing, such as being able to open them full-screen in a new tab in Firefox (you will have to have a video playing to use the maximize function, though). Install the script here http://userscripts.org/scripts/show/4703.

354 Virtual Video Map

Thanks to tagging, this is a cool mashup that enables you to view videos of specific areas. The videos are tagged and then displayed with markers via Google Maps. It's a neat example of what you can do when APIs are made available to developers, and is well worth a look.

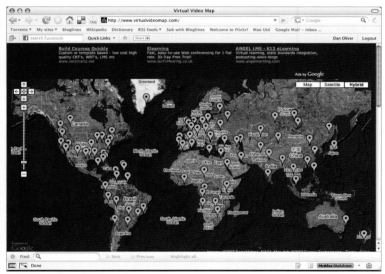

356 YouTube comments next to video

Just as it sounds, this script enables you to have comments displayed next to videos, so you don't have to scroll away from the clip to read what people have to say. As with all scripts, some will clash, so remember what you already have installed. Get the script at http://userscripts.org/scripts/show/7174.

357 Groups

If you have a specific interest and want to access videos about it, why not join a Group? Select the Community tab, hit the See More Groups link, and then use the category links on the left to narrow your search. When you find a group you like the look of, select the link and choose to Join This Group. New videos added to this Group will now appear on your Profile page.

355 YouTube Resizer

We're back in the realm of the Greasemonkey with this next tool. YouTube Resizer is a handy script that changes the size of the YouTube player, and places links, etc., below the video. Visit http://userscripts.org/scripts/show/3975 to install the script (see tip 040 on how to install Greasemonkey scripts).

Keep In Touch

We've already introduced you to the delights of Blogger, the number one tool for blogging, but it can take a lot of time maintaining such a presence. That's where Twitter can help. If you don't like the idea of a full-on blog, but want to keep friends updated with what you're up to, Twitter could be just what you've been looking for. Restricted to just 140 characters, Twitter enables you to indulge in micro-blogging via the Twitter site, from your cellphone, or via your favorite instant message (IM) client.

Twitter

358 Get started

The first thing you need to do is head over to www.twitter.com. Now select the Join For Free link to the right, and you'll be asked to provide some details (make sure you specify the right time zone). Once you've done this you'll be taken to the main Twitter page, but don't post yet.

359 Find and invite

Twitter is all about keeping friends and family up to speed with your latest news, so we need to add some people, and start following them. Select the Find & Invite link at the top of the site, and you'll be taken to a page where you can perform a number of different searches. Add a name to the Search box at the bottom of the page to see if they're already using Twitter.

360 Invite via email

If your friends aren't already using Twitter, or if you can't find them via the name search, then you can invite them to join, and search the existing Twitter email database. Select the Invite Via Email link from within the Find & Invite section, and you'll see a blank text field.

361 Use a CSV file

Now you can enter the email addresses of friends and family into the window (ensuring they are separated by commas) and hit Find/Invite. Most email applications enable you to export your address book as a CSV (comma separated values) file, which you can then copy and paste into this window. Mac users can use the excellent CSV exporter at http://www.apple.com/downloads/macosx/internet_utilities/addressbooktocsvexporter.html.

362 Gmail users

A relatively new feature to Twitter, and one that also makes Facebook so compelling, is the option to access your Gmail address book via Twitter. First you need to select the Find Folks From Your Gmail Address Book link, and then enter your Gmail details (don't worry, they're not stored). A list of your contacts already on Twitter will then be displayed (click them to start following). Select Next at the bottom of the screen, and you'll then be able to invite Gmail contacts.

363 Post an update

Now you have a few followers, people you've followed who have likely reciprocated, you can post an update. Select the Home link, and type what you're up to into the main text field, keeping it to 140 characters. When you're done, select Update. Many people call these updates Tweets.

364 Your Twitter home

Now, if you type www.twitter.com/YOURUSERNAME you'll be able to see your latest update. This is essentially your main blog page and you'll even find an RSS Feed link at the bottom, where people can subscribe to your updates. If you look to the top left, you'll see a box with Add A Photo inside; click the box. Now you can add a picture of yourself, with square dimensions being preferable.

365 Via cell

One of the main reasons why people love Twitter is that you can send and receive updates via your cellphone. To enable this function go to Settings, select Phone & IM, and add your cellphone number. A verification code will then be sent, which you should text back to 40404 from the US, and +44 7781 488126 from outside the US.

366 Turn off notifications

You'll receive a text message to validate that your cellphone is set up correctly. Although you can receive SMS/text updates every time someone you're following leaves a Twit, Tweet, or whatever you want to call it, it's best to turn this off (simply reply to the first text with OFF). The reason is that you're charged your network's rate for SMS messages, and they can add up. (If you have an unlimited SMS plan, you're fine!)

367 Send via text

Now that you've validated your cellphone number, and turned off notifications, you can send a Twitter update from your cell. This is a cinch to do, especially if you're living in the US. All US users need to do is text new updates to 40404. For international users, you'll have to text to +44 7781 488126 (we suggest adding Twitter as a contact in your phone, as it's a long number to remember).

368 Enable IM

To enable IM updates of Twitter go into your Settings, and select Phone & IM from the links at the top of the page. Twitter supports AIM, GTalk, .Mac, Jabber, and LiveJournal. If you use one of these IM clients, then select it from the drop-down menu, and enter your username in the text field beside it.

369 Verify IM

You'll now be taken to a page where you will need to verify your IM account. Select the link titled Click To Verify Your Account, and Twitter will then try and open your IM client automatically. A pop-up window will then appear, and you should choose Launch Application. Your verification code will now be added to your IM client, and all you need do is hit Send.

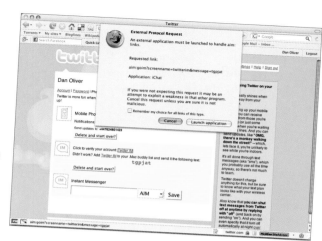

370 And finally

If you use GTalk, then you'll need to add twitter@twitter.com to your contacts, and send your verification code to that contact. Whichever client you're using, once you've entered your verification code you will then receive a message to confirm that your IM has been set up correctly. You will now be able to receive notifications via IM, but if you don't want all new Twitter notifications to be sent via IM you just need to send OFF via your IM client. To send new updates, just type them into your IM client. It's that simple.

371 Twitterific

Using Twitter via the main website is just fine, but there are stand-alone applications for both the Mac and PC that offer a great alternative to the website. We'll start by looking at Twitterific on the Mac. First, visit http://iconfactory.com/software/twitterrific/, and download the Twitterific software.

372 Launch Twitterific

When you launch Twitterific for the first time you will be prompted to provide your Twitter username and password. Once you've done this, you'll see the last few notifications displayed. A Twitterific logo will now appear in your system menu bar, which you select to toggle the application. To configure Twitterific select the spanner, select the "t" next to a Tweet to go to the author's homepage, and add new Tweets in the text box at the bottom of the interface.

373 Badges

You may remember that in the Flickr chapter we introduced you to the concept of badges. A badge is essentially a snippet of code that enables you to present content from one site on another. If you select the Badges link in Twitter, you'll see that you can post Twitter updates to MySpace, Facebook, Blogger, and TypePad. Select your preference, and you'll be guided through the installation.

374 Twitteroo

If you're using Windows, then you can keep updated with new Tweets via Twitteroo, a fantastic, stand-alone application for the PC. First, download the software from http://rareedge.com/twitteroo, then install and open the app. Add your username and password for Twitter, and select your notification preferences (such as color and frequency). Now you can easily post new Tweets, and see what others are up to.

375 Vista gadget

If you're running Windows Vista, and use the gadget sidebar, then there's a cool gadget that enables you to get the latest Tweets from Twitter. Go to http://arsecandle.org/twadget and select the download link. Open and install the gadget, select the spanner icon, and add your details.

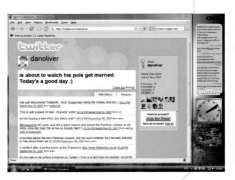

THE HENLEY COLLEGE LIBRARY

Gmail

As things currently stand, Gmail—or Google Mail, as it's also known—is the king of the free email providers. When it launched as a beta in 2004 it offered 1GB of free storage to users, compared to the few hundred megabytes offered by other well-known providers. With its Ajax-powered interface, Gmail quickly became the email provider of choice for geeks around the world. Now, with a free inbox of almost 3GB, Gmail is simply the best online email service available, geek or no.

378 Signature

For now we're going to look at using Gmail as your primary address. Before you start sending emails, you should make sure you have entered a signature, so that recipients of your emails have the right information (this is also a great place to promote your blog or website). In the General section of Settings scroll down to signature, and add the details you'd like displayed. Now just scroll down, and select Save Changes.

376 Get started

To get your free Gmail account, you need to visit www.gmail.com, and select the Sign Up For Gmail/Google Mail link. This will then take you to a page where you must specify your details, choose an email address, and then select a password. As you type your password, a Password Strength bar will indicate how appropriate your password is. Make sure it says Good before continuing.

377 Settings

Now you've signed up, you'll need to make a few changes in the settings section. Once you've signed in at www.gmail.com, you'll be taken to your inbox. In the top right of the interface you'll see your email displayed, with a Settings link next to it. Enter the Settings section.

379 Contacts

Before we go any further in the settings, let's take a step back and look at Contacts. If you look at the menu to the right, you'll see a Contacts link about halfway down. You can add individual contacts by using the Create Contact link, which, once selected, will take you to a screen where you can add their information, and even upload a picture.

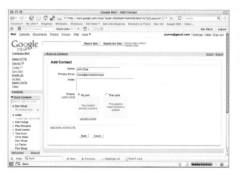

380 Import contacts

Adding contacts individually can take a long time, but if you already have a list of contacts from another mail client then it's easy to import them to Gmail. Firstly, select the Import link, in the top right on the Contacts section. Now you'll have to save your address book as a CSV file, browse to it, and select Import Contacts (full details on exporting CSV files are available by selecting the Learn More link).

381 Adding that image

To associate an image with your account, and to enable others to use it, you need to enter Settings, and in the General section choose Select A Picture. Find an image on your hard drive (ensuring it's a JPEG, BMP, GIF, or PNG file), select Upload Picture, then drag the crop area until it's right for you. Remember to Save Changes.

382 Where are my folders?!

It won't be long before you notice something rather unnerving about Gmail: it has no folders! For most of us, folders are an integral part of our email experience, and Gmail doesn't have any. However, in the next few steps we'll reveal why this doesn't actually matter.

383 Labels

Instead of folders, Gmail uses Labels. So rather than physically moving messages to a folder, you assign labels manually or automatically using Filters (which we'll look at shortly). We're going to create a Label that displays all messages that include attachments. Go to Settings, select Labels from the options, and create a new label called Attachments.

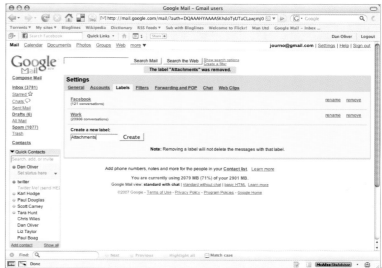

384 Labeling messages

Once you've created the Label, head back to your main Inbox. Now, whenever an email comes in with an attachment, you can attribute the relevant Attachments label to it by selecting it from the More Actions drop-down menu. You can then access all emails with this label via the Labels section on the right.

386 Applying a Label

In the next section, you'll see a number of choices. To have an email go straight to one of your Labels, select Skip The Inbox. In this instance we're going to uncheck Star It, go to Apply the Label, and check the box that applies it to all conversations (emails). The final step is to select Create Filter.

387 Why the Attachments Label?

We didn't just set up the Attachments label for illustration purposes; it actually serves as the best way of managing the size of your inbox. A limit of 3GB may seem astronomical and impossible to fill, but eventually you could. By labeling all mails with attachments, you can easily access and delete those messages taking up the most space in your inbox.

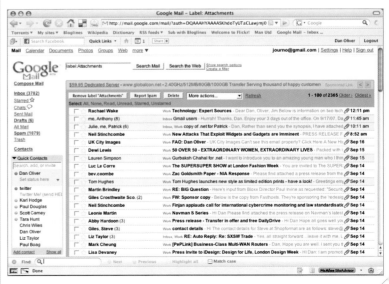

385 Filters

Labels are great, but they really become useful when you combine them with filters. For instance, let's take our Attachments label. At the moment, we have to manually add it to emails with attachments. However, if you go into Settings, Filters, select Create New Filter and you'll see a number of filter options (from sender, to subject, to keywords). Check the Has Attachment box, and select Next Step.

388 Star it!

Next to every email in Gmail is a little star icon, which can be selected and deselected at will. This is a quick way of flagging emails as important, or setting them aside to be actioned later (once starred, you can access any tagged email by selecting the Starred link on the left).

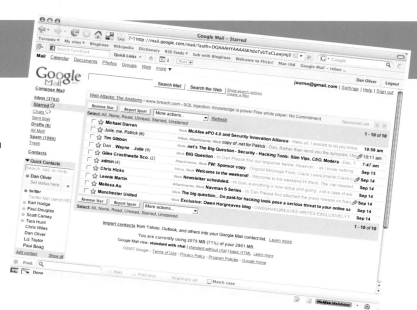

389 When to bypass the inbox

With our filter for the Attachments label, we wanted to keep all emails with attachments in the main inbox (not move them out). Sometimes, though, you'll want emails to skip your inbox. To do this, set up a Label as we did before, select Create A New Filter, then in the From window enter the email address updates are sent from (or a section of the address), and on the next screen select Skip Inbox.

390 Get notified!

When you start bypassing your inbox, it may become harder to know when new messages have arrived. To solve this problem, you can use a notification tool. You can download a great Firefox add-on at https://addons.mozilla.org/en-US/firefox/addon/173. Once installed, select the Gmail icon, add your account details, and you'll be notified of any new mails.

391 More on Notifier

To check out the preferences, scroll down to Add-Ons in the Firefox Tools menu, and select Preferences under Gmail Notifier. Here you can select how Gmail opens (in a new tab, for example), whether to show which label the mail is in, the option to play a sound alert, and all manner of other cool stuff.

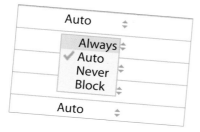

392 Quick Contacts

If you look to the left of the Gmail interface, you'll see a list of 10 names under the Quick Contacts heading. Your Quick Contacts list enables you to generate emails and start chat sessions with the people you email most. Select the Contacts link, search for a contact, and select Always from the drop-down on the right to promote someone to this section.

393 Get chatting

If you'd rather indulge in some instant messaging, then you can start a chat session with other contacts who are also logged in. You'll see a green dot next to any contact signed into Gmail, and can simply roll over their name in Quick Contacts to open a pop-up window. Select Chat in this window, and a conversation window will open.

394 Chat settings

Go into Settings and select Chat from the top menu. In this section you can decide whether you want to save your chat history, choose how many contacts you'd like to display in your Quick Contacts list, and select whether Quick Contacts appears above or below your Labels (we'd select Below). You can also have sounds play to notify you of new chat messages.

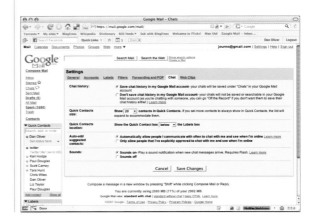

395 Web Clips

By default, you'll get little news stories, called Web Clips, which appear on your front page. These are sold as a benefit, but they're not really. To turn Web Clips off, go into the Settings section, select Web Clips, and uncheck the box at the top of the page. Now, when you go to your inbox, there won't be any external information at the top of the page.

398 Simple search

We couldn't talk about Gmail, without mentioning its fantastic search option. For a simple search just type what you're looking for into the Search Mail window at the top of Gmail. To get more control over a search, select Show Search Options.

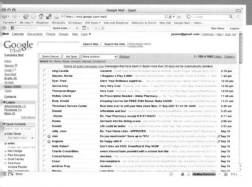

396 Gmail Spam

Spend any amount of time online and you'll become exposed to junk mail (also known as spam). As the world's biggest search engine, the guys at Google know their way around algorithms, and this means that when it comes to spam identification it doesn't get much better. We found no incorrectly identified spam messages in our Spam folder, but you can still access it should you wish to.

397 No Chat

Although a lot of people love Gmail's option to initiate chats with contacts, many don't. Thankfully, Google has taken this on board, and if you scroll to the bottom of the page you'll see a series of links under the title Google Mail View. Here you can choose Standard With Chat, Standard Without Chat, and Basic HTML.

399 Predicates

If you want even more control over searches, you can use specific predicates (tags you can apply that enable you to get certain data returned). First up, you can use "From:", "To:", and "Subject:" (so, for example, you could search for "from:dan oliver to:rotovision subject:book"). Other predicates include "Has:attachment", "Filename:", "Before:", "After:", "Label:", "CC:", and "BCC:". It takes some getting used to, but once you do you'll be hooked.

Gmail: take things further

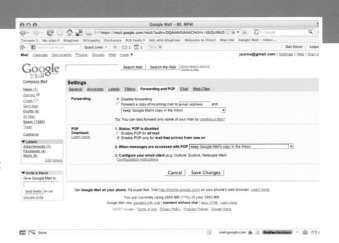

 Use POP

If you prefer to use an email client such as Apple Mail or Outlook Express then you can, as Gmail has POP support. To enable this, first you need to go into Settings, and select Forwarding and POP. Now select whether you want to enable POP for all mail, or just new mail (POP means mail will be downloaded to your Mac or PC, so choose wisely). Now select the drop-down, and choose if you'd like to keep copies of email in Gmail. Now save your changes.

Configure your client

Now you'll have to go into your mail client and create a new account. First, you need to note that Gmail's incoming mail server is pop.gmail.com, your username is your email address, and your password is your Gmail password. The outgoing mail server is smtp.gmail.com, and if you need to enter a port number then it's 587. If you need any further help, you can visit the Gmail Help Center at http://mail.google.com/support.

 Forwarding

If you simply want to forward emails to another account, then this is also a cinch to do. Go into Settings, select Forwarding And POP, and select the box that starts with Forward A Copy. Now place the email that you'd like your mail forwarded to in the opposite box, and then decide if you want the mail archived or deleted once it's been forwarded.

403 Vacation message

Under the General section in Settings you'll see a section called Vacation Responder. When people email, they expect a response. So, if you're going to be away for a few days, you can have a message automatically sent out to people. You can enter a subject, message contents, and also select whether you only want Contacts to receive the message. This is a good idea, for security reasons if nothing else.

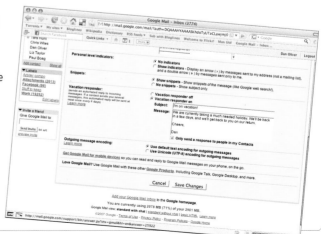

406 Print individual emails

This may not seem tricky, but a lot of people don't know that you can print individual emails without having to print out whole conversations. To do this, simply open the email that you want to print off within a conversation, and then select the little triangle next to the Reply button (at the top right of the message). Now scroll down, and select Print.

404 Drafts

If you're ever cut off in the middle of an email, or simply forget to actually send it, then Gmail will save a Draft copy of the email, which will then appear under Drafts in the menu on the left of the Gmail interface. This is useful for preparing emails that you may want to send at a later date, or need to get checked before sending.

407 Select all messages

When Gmail first launched, there was no way to select all messages in a mailbox or within a Label: this sucked. Clearing your account was a nightmare, and making wholesale changes a total drag. But lucky you, Google fixed this. To select all messages, first hit All next to Select (at the top of the interface). When you do this, a magic link will appear, giving you the option to select all conversations in the given section. Once you've selected this, you can then make changes to all the emails in a given area.

405 Keyboard Shortcuts

To enable shortcuts go into Settings, and third down in the General section select Keyboard Shortcuts On. The table below shows the top shortcuts you can use.

SHORTCUT	DEFINITION	ACTION
c	Compose	This creates a new message. <Shift> + c creates a new message in a new window.
k or j	Move to conversation	Use these keys to move back and forth between conversations. Hit enter to open a conversation.
n or p	Move to email	Use these keys to move between messages. Hit enter to expand or collapse the message.
r	Reply	Reply to message sender. <Shift> + r will open it in a new window.
a	Reply all	Reply to all. Pressing <Shift> + a will open in a new window.
f	Forward	This will forward your message.

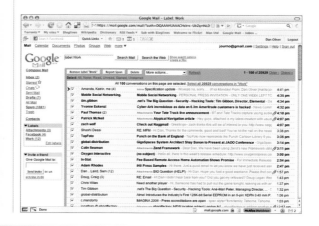

MySpace

MySpace may have fallen out of favor with many people, who have moved over to the likes of Facebook, but with 200 million accounts the site must be doing something right. Although MySpace caters to all users interested in social networks, and offers options such as video uploads and photo sharing, it has a specific interest for musicians who can upload up to four MP3s.

408 Get started

First, pay a visit to www.myspace.com, and select the Sign Up button on the right. As with most of the sites we've covered, you'll now have to provide personal information and specify which country you live in. At this point you should read the Terms and Conditions.

409 Add some pictures

In the next step of the sign-up process you'll be taken to a screen where you can upload pictures to your account. You'll only be able to upload one image at this stage using the upload tool, and although it's nice to get some stuff in your account before you get started, you can always add more later. At this point you can either select Skip For Now or you can navigate to an image, and upload it (there's a 5MB limit, and they must be JPEG or GIF files).

410 Adding friends

The next screen enables you to send out email invites to friends and ask them to join MySpace. Whether you opt to take advantage of this facility at this stage is down to how comfortable you feel bugging your friends and family. You can always do this at a later stage, so if you're in two minds, why not wait until you've finished signing up.

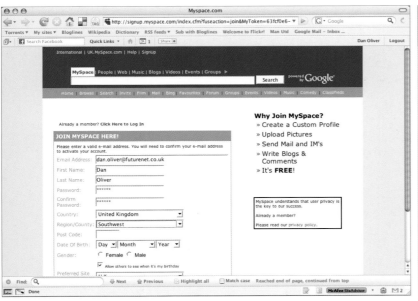

413 More profile information

While in the Edit Profile section you can also change your name, add basic details such as your height and body type (quite why you'd want to do this, we're not sure), and provide information on places you've studied and worked. Be careful when updating this section, and don't provide any details that you wouldn't offer up to a casual acquaintance.

411 Your home page

Next up, you'll be taken to your MySpace home page. The home page looks a little cluttered, so we'll take a few moments to highlight the different areas of the screen. At the top of the site is a search window, which enables you to search the content hosted on MySpace. Below that are links to your personal MySpace sections. Below that, to the left, is a box where you can edit your account.

414 Add contacts

Like Facebook, MySpace offers the option to search your email contacts in Yahoo, Gmail, and Hotmail, as well as enabling the upload of an existing address book. Scroll down your homepage, and on the right you'll see a box titled Search Your Address Book. Select your online mail provider, or Import Your Address Book.

412 Edit profile

Now would be a good time to provide a little more information on yourself–after all, that's what MySpace is all about. On your homepage, select the Edit Profile link in your profile section (where your picture is). On the next screen you can add a Headline, some About Me text, and other information on your interests, such as your favorite movies and music.

Search Your Address Book

See which of your friends are already on MySpace!

Find your **Yahoo, GMail,** and **Hotmail** friends on MySpace.

Import your address book.

417 Your URL

Now that you've set up your new URL, pay it a visit as this is what other users will see when they check you out on MySpace. You can now send this link to anyone who you want to share your profile with, and you'll see that the personal information you provided earlier is displayed, and that your profile picture is the one we uploaded when we were signing up. But that picture isn't really relevant, so let's sort that out.

415 Contacts continued

As we've just set up a Gmail account, we've chosen Gmail contacts to import. On the next screen MySpace requires that you enter your Gmail address and username. Following that, you'll be shown how many of your contacts have active MySpace accounts. By default they're unchecked, so go through and select the people you want to add to your friends.

418 Add new photos

Select Home from the links in the navigation bar. Now, in the profile section, select Upload/ Change Photos. From the buttons available on the next page, choose Upload Photos, and MySpace's upload tool will load up. By selecting Browse, you can now add multiple images. Hit Done, and your photos will upload (after which, you can give them titles).

416 Get a URL

OK, so we've sent out some invites, but it'll be a while until your friends approve your requests. In the meantime, let's set up our own MySpace URL (which will be the address of your blog). Under your Profile box there should be a link titled Pick Your MySpace Name/URL, which you need to select. Now you'll have to choose a MySpace name.

419 Set Default image

Changing your default MySpace image isn't as easy as it should be. First, you'll need to go to your homepage and select Upload/Change Photos. Now choose an album, and then click the image you'd like to use as your default. On the next screen you'll see a series of buttons above the image, the first of which is Set As Default, which you should now hit.

420 Add video

To add video to MySpace, first select the Add/Change Videos link. The next screen will be blank, but in the top right there's an Upload Videos button, which you need to click. Much like YouTube, you should now provide a title, description, and add relevant tags. Next you need to browse to your movie (there's a 100MB file limit), and select Upload.

421 Musicians on MySpace

If you're a musician and want to upload your music and information related to it, then you will have to set up a separate account. To set up a musician's account select the Music link and then choose Artist Signup on the next page. You can't switch back and forth between personal and musician accounts, so it's best to set up two separate accounts.

422 Modify your look

One of the defining factors of MySpace is the ability to change the look and feel of your Profile with HTML and CSS. To do this, select Edit Profile, and insert the necessary code in the About Me box:
1. Go to edit the "About Me" section of your profile.
2. Insert the following code, which is essential in order for your custom background to show up.

```
<style type="text/css">
table, td {
background-color:transparent;
border:none;
border-width:O;}
</style>
```

Although we've made the color "transparent" you can choose any web safe color. (You can find color codes at http://html-color-codes.com.) Leave it transparent if you want the background image to tile behind the whole page. If you want to use a picture as your background then you need to include the following snippet of code in between the <style></style> tags:

```
body{background-image:url("www.linktoyourimage.com");
background-attachment:fixed;}
```

Skype

There are few applications and sites that can take a big chunk of credit for getting people to move over to always-on broadband connections, but Skype is one such application. The ability to make free calls over the internet has helped revolutionize communications in recent years, and here we'll show you why.

423 Install Skype

Visit www.skype.com and download the application (the Skype site should auto-detect which operating system you are running). The site is also where you'll need to go to buy extra credit, but we'll look at that once we've walked through the basics. Once you start your download, you'll be redirected to a page that will take you through installation.

424 Start Skype

Having installed the application, a Skype window will open. Under the Skype Name field is a link titled Don't Have a Skype Name?, which you'll need to select. Now a new screen will open, where you will have to specify the username you would like, while also providing a password and contact email address. If your chosen username is available, you'll be signed in.

425 Skype details

A new window will automatically open once you sign in for the first time, where you can enter more details. These details include your full name, telephone numbers, web address, and picture. Only include what you're comfortable showing to your contacts. To add a photo, simply drag and drop it into the image window.

426 Blank box

Now, well, you'll just have a blank window on your screen. But before we start adding contacts, let's test the quality of our audio. To do this, select the Skype Test Call button under your name. A new window will open below the button, and you'll need to select the telephone icon, which will initiate a call and open a call window.

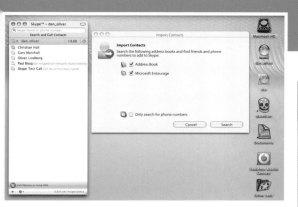

427 Add contacts

You can search for new contacts individually by selecting Contacts in the Skype menu, and then choosing Add A Contact. Alternatively, you can use an existing address book to cross reference the Skype database. Go to Contacts in the menu, scroll down to Import Contacts, and select your address book. Be aware, this can take a LONG time.

428 Chat

Skype isn't just about voice calls, as you can also use the software to instant message contacts. To do this, select a contact, and then select the little speech bubble by their name. This will open a chat window, and as well as sending text exchanges, you can exchange files with each other.

429 Conference call

A great option in Skype is the ability to initiate a conference call with up to nine people. To start your very own conference call, select Call from the Skype menu, and scroll down to Start Conference Call. In the new window that opens, highlight a name and hit Add To Conference. When you've added everyone, select Start.

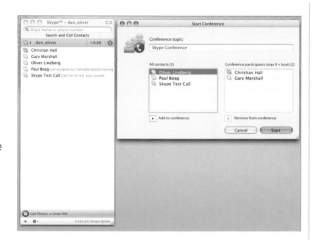

430 Buy more credits

Select Account from the menu, and scroll down to Go To My Account Page (this will sign you in at the Skype site). Now you can add credit to your account, so you're not limited to making calls to those people in your contacts, you can also call landlines at a fantastic rate. For more information visit http://www.skype.com/products/skypeout/rates/.

431 Avoid vishing

Yup, sad as it is, criminals are also using tools such as Skype to rip people off by "vishing" (making calls and requesting bank details, etc.). If you go to Skype>Preferences and select the Privacy tab, you can select who can make calls to you (such as limiting SkypeIn calls to your contacts).

meebo

Launched in September 2005, meebo is a website that enables you to connect to major instant messaging (IM) applications without having the software installed on your computer. This makes meebo a great alternative for travelers, students, office workers, and anyone else that needs quick access to instant messaging. meebo supports AIM, Google Talk, Yahoo!, MSN, ICQ, and Jabber, and in the next two pages we'll show you how to make the most of it.

432 Log on, sign in

To get started, head over to www.meebo.com. By default you'll see four instant messaging log-in screens on the left, with the meebo log-in on the right. Below the four instant message windows on the left you'll see a More Networks link, which exposes ICQ and Jabber. If you have your details, you can quickly sign in to any of the visible IM clients.

433 Sign up to meebo

With different friends using different IM services, meebo enables you to combine them all into one account. Select the Sign Up link under the meebo section on the right to get started. You'll have to choose a meebo identity and password, and enter your name, email, and age.

434 Manage accounts

With your meebo account, you're not just restricted to one IM client. Select an IM provider from the drop-down, enter your details, and check the box next to Add To My Meebo Account. Now sign in. All your contacts will show up in the window on the right. To send a message just double-click a name, and a new message window will open.

435 Add another account

To add contacts from another IM client, you will need to select the Accounts link. This will display all current accounts, but also features an Add Account button at the bottom of the account window. Select the Add Account button, and you set up another account (repeat this for each IM client you use).

436 meebo me

meebo would be a fantastic web application even if all it did was connect you to your IM accounts, but it does so much more. Via little bits of code called meebo me widgets, you can enable people that visit your site or blog to instant message you. Select the Meebo Me Widgets link to get started. Give the widget a name, choose a size, and select Show Preview. Finally, select Create A New Widget.

437 Widget code

Next up you'll be presented with a chunk of code that you'll need to paste into your blog or website; copy it. We've already created a Blogger site, so we'll show you how to add the code to a blog. Sign into Blogger, and head over to the Layout section. Select the Add A Page Element link, and choose HTML/JavaScript. Now paste the meebo code into this window, and select Save Changes.

438 Preferences

In the Preferences section you can change the way meebo looks and behaves, with the option to decide whether sounds will be played, pick a stylish skin, decide on whether emoticons display, and select whether chats are saved in your IM history. Within the Preferences section you can also amend Accounts and your widgets.

439 Change your icon

You can easily change your meebo icon to one of a selection of predesigned alternatives, and you can also upload your very own icon. To change your meebo icon you first need to select the icon next to the meebo welcome message on the left of the interface. Now scroll down to a new icon, or select Custom Icon at the bottom of the window, which will enable you to browse to an image on your hard drive (remember, there's an 80KB size limit).

Get Organized

In the last few years the sophistication of web-based applications has reached a point where they have now become serious alternatives to traditional desktop applications. More and more, people are asking themselves why they should pay hundreds of dollars for software, when there are web alternatives available for free. In this chapter, we're going to reveal just a few of the best web applications for getting yourself organized.

Google Calendar

440 Why Google Calendar?

Despite a number of fantastic online calendars being available–the most notable being 30 Boxes at www.30boxes.com–we've opted to cover Google Calendar. The reason is simple: Google Calendar ties in with Gmail and provides a great introduction to online calendars. If it doesn't suit, you can always try 30 Boxes, as they're both free!

441 Sign in

Because you've already signed up for a Gmail account, you'll automatically have access to Google Calendar (or Gcal, as we'll call it from now on). To access Gcal simply log in to Gmail, and select the Calendar link at the very top of the page; you'll now see a traditional calendar view. To add an entry, you just click the time on screen and give the entry a title. When you're done, select Create Event.

442 Event details

If you'd like to edit an entry further–with reminders, or by inviting guests–select the Edit Event Details link before hitting the Create Event button (although you can always add more details later). You'll now be taken to a screen where you can edit a number of details. Firstly, there's an All Day checkbox. If you're adding an event such as a vacation, then checking All Day will enable you to span an event from one date to another.

443 Repeats

If you have an event that will repeat, then you can select a frequency from the Repeats drop-down. Once you've done this, a number of new options will be displayed, such as how long you want the repeated event to continue for. You can also provide information on where the event will be, and add a description.

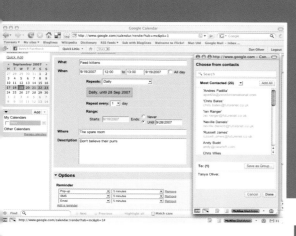

444 Guests and reminders

On the right you'll see a box titled Guests. You can either type the email addresses of people you'd like to invite to an event into this box, or select Choose From Contacts to add existing contacts. Scroll further down the page, and you'll also see a number of reminders you can choose (Pop-up, SMS, and email).

446 SMS reminders

To receive SMS reminders of Gcal events, you'll have to activate your cellphone number. To do this, you'll need to select Settings from the top right of the page, and then choose Mobile Setup. Before you start, you should check whether your carrier is supported. Once you've checked, you'll need to add your number. You'll then get an SMS message with a validation code, which you'll need to enter in the Verification Code box. You'll be charged your provider's standard SMS rate.

445 Display and edit

You will now be taken back to your calendar, where you'll see your new event. If at any point you want to edit an event, just select it in the main calendar view, and click the Edit Event Details link. However, if you only want to move the time then just drag the event, or to extend the duration you can drag the bottom of the event box. Select the tabs at the top of the calendar to get different views of your events.

447 Calendar options

Your calendar is displayed in a box on the left of the interface, with the title My Calendars. If you select the little arrow next to your calendar, you can change the color of all events added to that calendar (we'll explain why this is important later), change the details for this calendar (such as time zone), and if you select Share This Calendar, then you can make it available to others.

448 Notifications

The last option in the My Calendars drop-down menu is Notifications. In this section you can specify how you'll be reminded of calendar events, and for what kind of events you'll be notified. At the moment you can only have your daily Agenda sent to your Gmail address.

450 Quick Add

Below the Google Calendar logo you'll see two links: Create Event and Quick Add. When you select Quick Add, a new window pops up, and you can enter a line of text, which will instantly add a new event. You must fill in details in the following order "what," "who," "where," and "when" (though "what" and "when" is the only required information). So "meeting with Dave at the bar on Thursday at 1pm" is instantly added. If the place is called something like "The 3pm Bar," though, then it needs to go in quote marks.

449 Manage calendars

After a while, you may want a calendar for work, one for home, and maybe one for another member of the family. To add a new calendar, select the Manage Calendars link at the bottom of the My Calendars box. Now choose Create New Calendar. You'll have to provide a name (and a description if you wish), as well as choosing a time zone, and deciding whether you'll share the calendar. Hit Create Calendar when you're done.

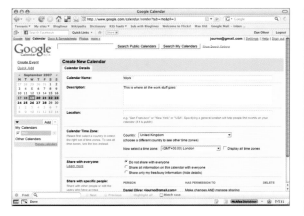

451 Add to a specific calendar

Now you have a few different calendars, you can easily specify which calendar a new event should be attributed to. When you create a new event, a new drop-down menu will now appear called Which Calendar, and you can select your calendar of choice from this menu.

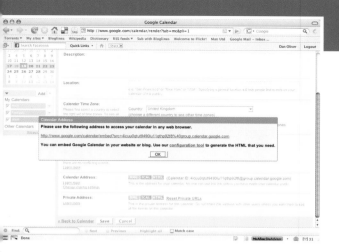

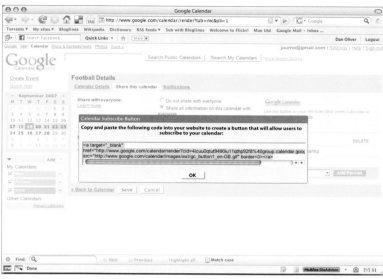

452 Going public

If you have a specific calendar that you'd like to share with others–such as a club calendar–then you can do so. Go to Settings>Calendars, and select one of your calendars. Now go to Share This Calendar and enable sharing. Finally, scroll down to Calendar Address in Calendar Details, and you'll see three buttons (XML, ICAL, and HTML). Selecting XML will provide a link for feed readers, choose ICAL for inclusion in Apple's iCal calendar, and HTML is a direct link to a webpage.

453 Embed calendar

When you select the HTML button, you'll see a link that enables you to embed a calendar in your site or blog; select the Configuration Tool link. On the next page you can set the appearance of your calendar and you'll be presented with the code, which you'll need to paste into your blog or website.

454 Share a calendar

If you go to Share This Calendar in your calendar settings, you'll now see a little Google Calendar button on the right. If you select the Get The Code link, then you'll be presented with a chunk of code that you can put on your site, which will then display a button that users can click to subscribe to your calendar.

455 Search

Because it's so easy to publish your calendars, there are public calendars that you can easily subscribe to (for TV shows, sporting fixtures, etc.). Type what you're looking for in the search window, select the Preview link of one of the returned calendars, and if you like what you see then select the Add Calendar button. This will now be listed under Other Calendars in your My Calendars box.

Google Docs

Google has spent a lot of time and money in a bid to break Microsoft's stranglehold on office tools, and now it can boast a fantastic web-based alternative to Microsoft Office: Google Docs. And best of all, it's totally free (and by the time you read this, according to Google, there should also be desktop versions that you can install). So, whether you're an intrigued Microsoft Office user looking for a change, or someone that's new to office tools, we think you'll be impressed with what Docs has to offer.

456 Documents

Sign into your Gmail account, and have a look at the links at the top of the page. Click the Documents link, and a new tab should open in your browser. Within this tab you should now see a pretty stark interface, but we'll soon sort that out. At the top of the interface you'll see a series of buttons. Select New, and scroll to Document.

457 Edit window

You'll now be taken to an edit screen, which will be familiar to anyone who's used a word processing package before. Above the main text you'll see a series of icons that enable you to control font appearance, lists, alignment, and style. Docs even auto saves as you go, should you forget to do so.

458 Spelling

If you look at the bottom of the Docs interface, you'll see a Spelling link. Selecting this link will, not surprisingly, check the spelling within your document, but if you select the little arrow next to the link, you can set the dictionary to your country of origin. Next time you log into Docs, this spelling preference will have been saved, so you only have to change it once.

459 File menu

If you look to the top left, you'll see the File menu. Select this and a drop-down menu will appear, with the option to save your document and export in a number of formats, including Word and PDF. You can also check word counts, and find and replace text.

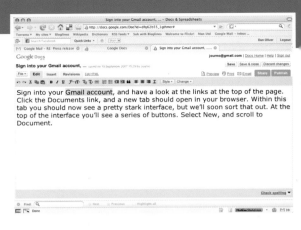

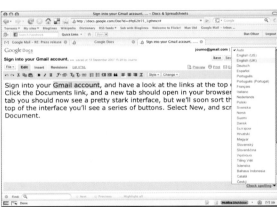

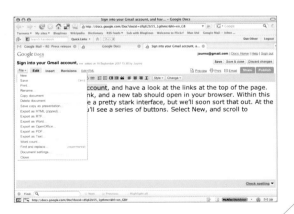

460 Document settings

In the File menu, select Document Settings; a new window will now open. At the top of the box is the option to turn off all styles if you wish to, and below that you can set a font and point size for all future documents. You can also set line spacing, and change the default background color. Once you've made your selections, check the box to make these settings your Default.

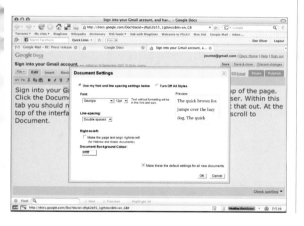

461 Insert

If you select the Insert tab above your document, you can add elements such as images, tables, comments, links, bookmarks, and separators. When you insert an image, you can resize it proportionally by holding <Shift>, and dragging a corner. If you insert a Comment, just click it with your mouse to delete it, or change its color.

462 Sharing

The great thing about a web-based office tool is the ability to share and collaborate. To share a document with others, select the Share tab on the right. You can invite people as Collaborators (who can edit) and Viewers (who can just see the document). To invite contacts, either type in comma-separated addresses, or click the Choose From Contacts link (remember to select Invite). If you don't want those you invite to be able to invite others, then uncheck Collaborators May Invite Others.

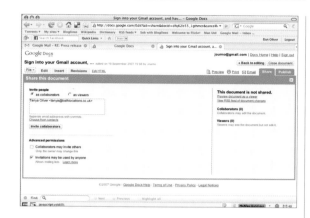

463 Revisions

Any changes made to the document will show up under the Revisions tab, which becomes important when sharing documents with others. If you want to compare differences between two documents, you can check the box next to a state, and hit the Compare Checked box. You can also access and edit the document in any one of its revised states.

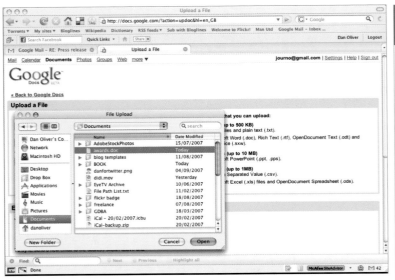

466 Spreadsheets

Now let's look at Google Docs' spreadsheet support. Go to New>Spreadsheet, and a new sheet will open. As with word processing, those of you with Office will be familiar with the layout of the interface. You can create static spreadsheets in Docs or, using the Sort and Formulas tabs, you can perform calculations on your spreadsheets.

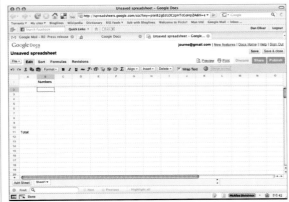

464 Upload

Now select Save & Close, and you'll be taken back to the main Docs screen. Thanks to Docs supporting a number of formats, you can also upload existing documents, so you can access them online. Select the Upload tab, and then navigate to the file you'd like to upload on your hard drive (supported files include .doc, .txt, .xls, .ppt, and .pps).

467 Simple Formula

It's not difficult to grasp spreadsheet basics. In your spreadsheet create a column called Numbers, and place a few numbers in it. Now write Total where you'd like these figures to be added together. Select the Formulas tab, select the Sum link on the right, now select the first number, hold <Shift>, select the last number, and hit <Enter>. This column's contents will now be added together. Easy, eh? If this has made you want to learn more about spreadsheets, pay a visit to http://spreadsheets.about.com.

465 Email documents

While still in the Upload section, scroll down the page and you'll see a long email address that finishes "writely.com." Any message sent to this email will be automatically added to your documents, and the subject of that email will become the file name.

468 Presentation

In the main Docs interface go to New and scroll down to Presentation. On the next screen you'll be greeted by an interface split into two. On the left you can see a preview of your first slide, with a bigger version–which you can edit–on the right. In our example presentation, we'll keep things simple. To add a new title and subtitle, select the text, and enter your own (you can change the font attributes using the tabs at the top of the interface).

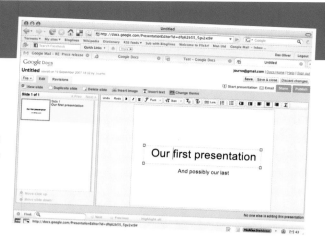

469 Themes

At the moment our presentation is a bit bland, but Docs provides a few tasteful themes to choose from. Select the Themes tab, and a new window will appear that features the themes you can choose from. We've opted for Gradient Black. Now we can start adding some new slides, which you do by selecting the New Slide link to the top left of the interface.

470 New slide layout

When you select the New Slide option, you'll be presented with five different layouts. If you want to keep things looking as tidy as possible and are new to presentations, stick with the preformatted columns. As with the first slide, just select inside an area to add text. To add an image, select Insert Image from the top layer of tabs, and navigate to the image you'd like to add (there's a 2MB size limit).

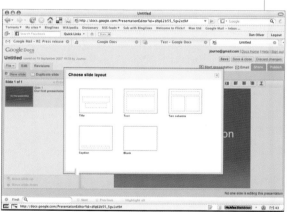

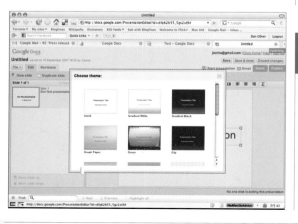

471 Present online

A fantastic aspect of Docs is the ability to share your presentation online. To do this select Start Presentation, which will kick your presentation into full screen. At the top right is a link, which you can then distribute to others online. As they join, they'll appear in the Audience window, and when all are assembled, you can start your presentation.

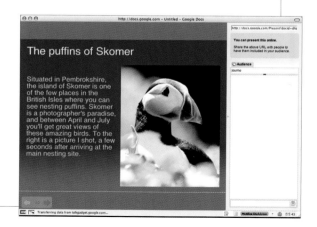

Stikkit

Stikkit is a site that enables you to keep all your daily jottings in one place and have them connect over time. While physical memo notes simply scatter your information around your desk, Stikkit makes connections between them, and provides structure and relationships to your notes. This is a great way to bring together the flotsam and jetsam of information that we collect on a daily basis, so let's get started!

472 Sign up

First, head over to www.stikkit.com, and select the Stikkit For Free link to the right. Once you've provided details, you'll be taken to the Stikkit interface, where there will be sample "stikkits" to look at (you won't need these, so delete them by hovering over the stikkit and clicking the trash can).

473 Tabs

Across the top of the Stikkit interface are a series of tabs. From left to right they are home (Ctrl + 1), stikkits (Ctrl + 2), calendar (Ctrl + 3), to-do list (Ctrl + 4), peeps (Ctrl + 5), bookmarks (Ctrl + 6), tags (Ctrl + 7), history (Ctrl + 8), and lastly, new stikkit (Ctrl + n).

474 New stikkit

To add a new stikkit you can either select the New Stikkit icon, which is the tab on the far right of the top menu, or you can press Ctrl + n. This will open a new window. To illustrate how Stikkit works, start typing someone's name into the note and a little Thinking symbol will start to flash.

475 Thinking

The thing that sets Stikkit apart from other online note applications is its ability to think. By "think," we don't mean it'll play you at chess, but it will start to identify the context of your notes. Try typing a phone number under the name you've just typed, and the note will change color. Because it includes contact information, this note is now a Peep. Hit Save, or Ctrl + s.

476 Peeps

You'll now see that your Stikkit has been saved as a Peep (a contact). Because Stikkit is based in the US, the prefix on all phone numbers defaults to +1. If you need to change this, go back into your Peep (Ctrl + e) and place +## (replacing # with the country code) in front of the number. This will override the US default.

i this stikkit's aka is "tanya"

✉ you can send email to this stikkit at
tanya0922@ahdanielsan.stikkit.com

⚡ email notification of changes and comments is **OFF** (click to turn on)

478 The power of aka

Let's say that you'd like to arrange a meeting with one of your contacts in Stikkit. Create a new stikkit, and write something like "Lunch meeting at 2pm with (the name of your contact)." As you type, Stikkit will start thinking. First, Stikkit will note that you've written 2pm, and add it to your schedule for that day (provide a day or date to be more specific). Next up, Stikkit will recognize the aka of your contact. Save this stikkit.

477 Top line and aka

Whenever you create a new stikkit, the first line will become the title of your stikkit. Also, you'll notice that your stikkit will be given an "aka" (in our example, it's "Tanya," because that's the first word we typed). While writing a stikkit if you type "aka" followed by a word, that word will overwrite the default and become the "aka" for that stikkit (we've changed ours to "tan"). But what's the point of these aka things?

479 Related stikkits

Now, head over to the Peeps section, and select the contact you just referenced in your appointment stikkit. Look to the right, and you'll see that the appointment you just added has shown up under Related Stikkits.

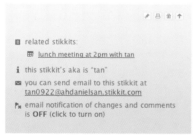

480 Tags and to-dos

When you create a stikkit, if you add a new line that starts "tag as," then you can specify tags for individual entries, enabling you to group and search them later. Lastly, if you'd like to create a new to-do item, use words such as "get," "buy," or "make." Also, you can use "+" and "-". To truly appreciate Stikkit you need to use it, so get cracking!

Get Paid

In the next four pages we're going to reveal the top 20 websites you can use to make some money on the net—with the minimum amount of effort. These sites range from ways to make money from advertising, to those that enable you to cash in on your photos and videos. Whatever you're doing online, there are always ways to make a few extra bucks.

The top money-making websites

 Revver

While YouTube may be the king of online video, it's Revver (www.revver.com) that's blazed the trail when it comes to making money from your videos. Upload a video at Revver, and you'll get 50 percent of the advertising revenue generated by said video. If you're going to upload a video and think it could be a success, then Revver could be worth a shot.

 eBay

It's the daddy of auction sites, and millions of people swear by eBay. Sometimes in the press for the wrong reasons, you shouldn't be put off using eBay to sell your unwanted goods, as the vast majority of transactions are trouble-free. Follow eBay guidelines, and you'll find the experience much more pleasurable (http://pages.ebay.com/help/tp/isgw-buyer-protection-steps.html).

483 Google AdSense

If you have a site or blog, then Google AdSense (www.google.com/adsense) enables you to place a piece of code on your site, which will serve contextual ads to your visitors based on your site content. You may not make enough to quit your job, but if you have a good amount of traffic it could be fruitful.

484 Google Video

Despite Google's dominance of online advertising, it doesn't seem to have gotten its head around video just yet. You can sort out revenue share with videos uploaded to Google video, but the Sponsored Videos scheme (www.google.com/adsense) is only available to a limited number of uploaders.

485 Flixya

We're still concentrating on video, and would like to direct you to Flixya (www.flixya.com). Like Revver, all you need to do is upload a video, get some serious traffic, and then you can enjoy a 50/50 ad revenue share with the producers of the site.

486 Scoopt

There's been a lot of buzz around the term citizen journalism, and what it means for the future of reporting on the web. What with cellphones that record video and take pictures, and a host of free blogging tools, anyone can now have a go at capturing news events. And if you get any cool photos on your travels, get in touch with the guys at Scoopt, and they'll sell them on (giving you a cut, obviously).

487 SpyMedia

From the name of the site, you can probably guess that it has much in common with Scoopt. Spot a celebrity doing something they shouldn't, and these guys will buy the photographic evidence. Charming.

488 BlogBurst

If you don't fancy stalking minor celebrities with a camera phone, why not try syndicating your blog content? BlogBurst syndicates blog entries to organizations such as Reuters, USA Today, and FoxNews, and the top 100 users get paid between $50 and $1,500 per quarter.

490 HubPages

HubPages (www.hubpages.com) is a site where you can share advice, reviews, useful tips, and anything else you like, with other web users. When people click on adverts within your hub you'll make some cash. Sign up is free, and if you think you can develop a strong community, it's worth a shot.

489 PayPerPost

PayPerPost is a company that pays you to blog about certain products or subjects. If you think this is a sure fire way to guarantee that your blog loses all credibility, then you'd be right. However, you may not care a jot, and if that's the case then this could be a good way to pull in some extra coin.

491 Grooveshark

If you're a music lover, then Grooveshark (http://grooveshark.com) could be the web application for you. This app enables you to access and share DRM-free music, and be rewarded for the music you produce or listen to. Registration is free, so there's nothing stopping you trying the service out.

$

492 ReviewMe

Another service that enables you to get paid for reviewing products on your blog, ReviewMe will put you in touch with companies that will then pay you to post reviews. This service is seen by many as being more ethical than some reviews sites out there.

493 Associated Content

Whatever the content you're producing—whether it be text, video, images, or audio—Associated Content (www.associatedcontent.com) enables you to upload that content, and then share in any revenue generated by selling it on to a third party. The site calls itself "The People's Media Company," and has a vociferous fan base.

494 RateItAll

Join the RateItAll community (www.rateitall.com), and make some cash from your recommendations. Having recently launched a beta version of a rewards program—called "The RateItAll Economy"—you can make money by writing a review and sharing in the generated ad revenue.

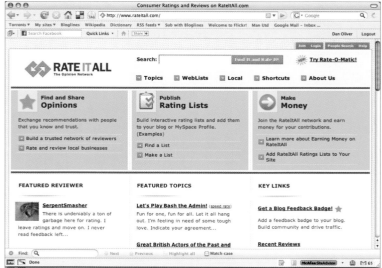

495 Gather

Gather (www.gather.com) enables you to create your very own online community, and share in any subsequent advertising revenue that's generated by the content in that group. You are also rewarded for using the site more actively.

496 Squidoo

Squidoo (www.squidoo.com) is one of the simpler and better executed sites for making a bit of extra cash. You create a single page—called a Lens—that then links out to blogs, links, feeds, auctions, products, whatever! Anytime someone buys a product through your Lens, or clicks a Google ad, you get 50 percent.

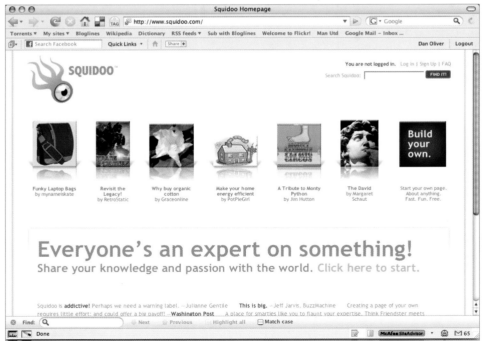

497 TutorLinker

If you're an expert in a given field, and like the idea of passing on your knowledge to others, then TutorLinker (http://tutorlinker.com) could be for you. You'll then be able to offer your services locally, and pull in some extra greenbacks.

498 iStockphoto

If you have the photography bug, and your pictures get others talking, why not register yourself at iStockphoto (www.istockphoto. com). Every time someone buys one of your images, you'll get a cut.

499 Newsvine

Another site that offers revenue share for writers–and it's one of our favorites–is Newsvine (www.newsvine.com). Newsvine brings together news from both traditional outlets and bloggers.

500 Daytipper

Last, but by no means least, is Daytipper (www.daytipper.com). Daytipper enables you to submit useful tips and get paid $3 for every one that gets added to the site. If you've got a hot tip burning inside you, this is the place to let it out!

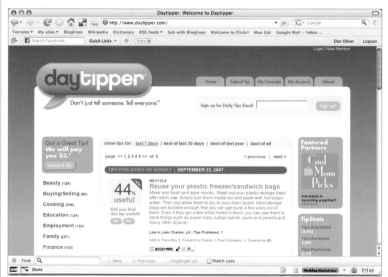

Glossary

Aggregator

An aggregator, also known as a feed reader, is an application (web-based or otherwise) that enables you to easily access syndicated web feeds via one interface, making it much easier to access the information you're interested in. Google Reader and Bloglines are among the most popular aggregators.

API

API is an acronym for application programming interface. In essence, this is a piece of code that enables requests for information from an outside source to be processed (so one site can request information from another by utilizing its API).

Blog

The word "blog" is a portmanteau of "web log." Blogs are sites that usually present information in a chronological order, and often contain personal accounts, written in the first person.

DRM

Digital rights management is a catch-all term used to describe the technologies that publishers are currently using to limit the use of their content. Famous proponents of DRM include Apple (via Fair Play on its iTunes Store) and Microsoft (via Windows Media Digital Rights Management).

Feed reader

See Aggregator.

FTP

This stands for File Transfer Protocol, which is a protocol for exchanging files over any network that supports TCP/IP (the communication protocols on which the internet runs).

HTML

HTML is an acronym for hypertext markup language, which is the predominant language used to create websites. HTML is defined using tags, which surround content on a website, and dictate how it will be presented.

Moblogging

This is the term to describe the act of blogging on the move, usually via a cellphone. The popularity of moblogging has increased with the rising penetration of smart phones and PDAs.

Open source

Most commonly applied to software, open source applies to code which has been created for use by the general public, with relaxed or nonexistent intellectual property applied to it. Open source projects often result in thriving communities, who feed back into the original code to improve it further.

Phishing

Phishing is the act of fraudulently trying to acquire personal information (such as name, address, bank details), and is usually in the form of an email which has been designed to look like it comes from a bona fide company.

POP

POP is an acronym for post office protocol, which is an internet protocol used to fetch email from a web connection. To be more specific, most people are talking about POP3 (the latest version of the protocol) when they discuss POP. In general, if you use POP with your email you will download messages from the server, and if you use the IMAP protocol then you generally leave messages on the server.

RSS

This is an acronym for really simple syndication and is used to describe a group of web feed formats, which enable you to publish regularly updated content such as blog posts and news stories to the web, and have others notified of any new content that's published. Although there are other feed syndication specifications, such as Atom, RSS has become a catch-all term among many web users to describe feed syndication.

Social bookmarking

This term is used to describe the sharing of bookmarks with other users on the web. There are a number of tools to help facilitate social bookmarking, the most notable of which is del.icio.us.

Social network

The term social network is used to describe sites such as MySpace and Facebook, where users connect to create communities based around friendships, common interests, and other factors.

Spam

In a web context, spam is generally used to describe unsolicited communication, most notably received via email. The etymology of spam is debatable, but the most credible theory is that it came from the Monty Python comedy sketch, where characters repeatedly use the word.

Tag

A tag can either refer to a piece of HTML or—especially in the Web 2.0 world—it applies to a keyword associated with a piece of content (whether it be a video, link, photo, or audio file).

Tweet

An apt word to describe an update on the popular micro-blogging service that is Twitter.

User interface

Also known as the HMI, or human machine interface, the user interface is the thing that enables you to interact with and control a site, machine, device, or other tool. In this book, we talk about the user interface with regards to software packages and websites.

Vishing

This term is a portmanteau of "voice" and "phishing", and is used to describe the illegal practice of using Voice over IP (VoIP) to get hold of someone's personal data.

VoIP

Voice over internet protocol doesn't really trip off the tongue, so say hello to VoIP (pronounced vo-y-p). This is the protocol for telephony over the internet, which enables the transfer of voice signals over IP, and is the reason why millions of people are now using software such as Skype to keep in touch with friends and family.

Web 2.0

This is a term that has been used to collectively describe sites and services that make up the second generation of the net. Web 2.0 is used to describe sites and services that enable collaboration and sharing.

Web browser

A web browser is your window to the web, making sense of all the code and protocols that websites are built on. While Internet Explorer continues to be the king of the browsers, other offerings such as Firefox, Safari, and Opera have vociferous support among their respective users. Firefox is regarded by many to be the best browser out there, with better support for web standards.

Index

Acknowledgments

I would like to thank you for purchasing this book. I hope that you've found it to be a useful guide through the choppy waters of the net, and that it's gone some way to making your life online a more pleasurable one.

I would also like to thank the following people for their help while producing this book: Gary Marshall, Richard Stevenson, Yura Smolsky, Anthony House, and from RotoVision, Jane Roe, Liz Farrelly, and Tony Seddon.

Finally, I owe a special thank you to Tanya, the love of my life, for her continued support and fortitude.